"Food is our common ground, a universal experience."

James Beard

Introduction

The food we eat matters. It does. It matters.

The line here is pretty clearly drawn: either you believe this, that the food we eat matters, that it has a real, tangible effect on our health and well being, and more importantly, on that of our children, or you don't.

If you don't, I implore you to read on, so that I can convince you that it does.

If you do, if you believe that there is a link between the food that we, as a nation, are consuming and our declining health, but don't quite understand what has happened to our food and what we can do about it, please, don't put this book down.

If you believe that the food we eat matters, and understand why, and get what your kids should and shouldn't be eating but are at a complete loss as to how to get there from here, keep reading, because THE FOOD WE EAT MATTERS.

The sad fact is that conventional food today is not satisfying the nutritional needs of our children. These are needs, not wants. Kids need food. Real food. They need it now more than ever. This generation that has been raised on processed foods is the least healthy, lowest achieving generation in our nation's history.

That's bad news.

Here's the good news: it's an easy fix. Well, not hard, anyways. Maybe a little bit awkward at first, at times more cumbersome, but honestly, you can feed your families healthy, real food, without a major expense of time or money. And the benefits…well, intelligent, healthy, productive children are what we hope for, and the food we feed them increases the degree to which they achieve these potentials. Seriously. The food that children eat affects how smart, productive and capable they become. There, I said it. It really does. They don't just need to be filled when they eat. They need to be nourished.

Making the switch away from processed yuck to real food may seem daunting at first, but it's necessary, and totally worth it. I'm not going to lie: it takes some work, some adjusting. It might not be as easy as a fast food life. Easy can sometimes be great, but at what price?

Children need good health. They need to be firing on all cylinders each day. It's our job, as parents, to enable them. This simple thing, providing them with good health, will prove to mean far more than any soccer practice or music lesson or video game, and some day they will thank you for attending to their nutritional needs, even if it meant making a few sacrifices. And really, feeding our children should not be an inconvenience or an afterthought. It should be our top priority.

The bottom line is, conventional processed food is crap. It's an amalgamation of highly processed wheat, soy and corn that has no nutritional value whatsoever. It's synthetic goo.

It's affecting our kids, and some changes need to be made. The changes are do-able, and they're vital. We need our children to go to school nutritionally capable of all that is being asked of them.

Children need real food. What they're getting now isn't cutting it.

Get Your
Kids
Off
Crap

The Hows and Whys
of the
REAL FOOD REVOLUTION

This book is the result of an eight year endeavor that involved cooking lunch for children. It is intended as a guideline, a means of making some changes in the way you feed your families. It is not a medical journal, and I am not a doctor. Nor am I a scientist. I did not perform any tests, qualitative or quantitative, before writing this book. I'm sharing with you some of my opinions and recipes. I'm not offering medical advice. Any product, company or organization mentioned in this book is done so without endorsement. The websites and sources that I've noted were accurate and correct when this book went to print.

Thank you, thank you, thank you,

Cathy. You've lifted us up.

Karen. For everything.

Jenna. More than every drop of water on every blade of grass

I was watching a late night talk show recently when a prominent mayor of a large city said "our children are being sent to school nutritionally unfit to learn." He made the comment in passing, and it went unanswered. When he said it, I sat bolt upright and literally yelled at my TV "don't just pass that over!" This is the crux of the situation in America today. **Our children are being sent to school nutritionally unfit to learn**. And that's a crying shame.

I know that there are many of you who are putting this book down now, because you don't believe all this hoopla about the state of today's food. For your child's sake, please don't. There really is a food crisis in America today.

Here's why: today's food barely qualifies as food. And people need food. The nutrients that are supposed to be in the food (like minerals and fats and proteins and vitamins) are necessary. The human brain must have nutrients to function. And the processed stuff that we are consuming, en masse, is not real food, and does not contain the things we need to thrive. It's filler. Conventional, processed foods may be edible and look like food, but in essence, they bear little resemblance to the real thing.

This is not just hippie hype. When the entities that conspired to create this stuff that we are eating in such abundance did so it was with profit, and not the health of a nation, in mind. As a result our children are not being nourished the way that they should be, and I believe it shows. This food crisis, be it by cause or by effect, is unfolding at a critical juncture in American history. I think we're going to need this generation to be healthy, and we're going to need it to be smart.

And who am I? Why should you care what I think? Am I some kind of expert?

Sort of.

As owner and operator of Real Meals Food Company, a one-person operation dedicated to the pursuit of serving real food, specifically to school children, I cook all-natural, from-scratch, mostly organic, always completely REAL lunches at a small private school in Michigan. I've been doing this for eight years, and we (my daughter and myself) have been eating only real food for six.

I had spent a good twenty years in the food and beverage industry before becoming a lunch lady, working in every capacity from waitress to Director of Operations. When I first started cooking real lunches it was at a Waldorf school under the tutelage of the most wonderful natural kind sweet organic person, Shana, who moved to Australia after our first year of cooking lunches together. I learned a lot from her, and from Waldorf in general. For those of you who are unfamiliar with this movement, it's a very organic, natural approach to education and to childhood.

My daughter had attended this Waldorf school for a few years prior to my taking on the hot lunch gig, but I was really not completely indoctrinated into the organic lifestyle, and was, in fact, pretty oblivious to food issues. I did make my daughter's baby food, (highly recommended and not at all hard) and keep her "sugar-free" but when I began this hot lunch venture I had no idea what high fructose corn syrup or hydrogenated oils were, and assumed that if food was FDA approved it was, well, food.

I serve lunches on a per-order basis, and not everyone orders hot lunch. There are still a few parents who send the typical conventional fare in their kids' lunchboxes, and though the school is trying to move towards healthier choices as a whole, candy and crap still show up, much to the teachers' chagrin.

Hot lunches cost $6.50 each, and I know that might seem exorbitant to you. This is in part because school lunches are typically so cheap. More money needs to be spent on school lunch programs. You can't feed a child for one dollar. School lunch should not be a throw away. It should certainly, at the very least, be real food. Real food costs a little more money, but those costs are retrievable on the other end, in healthcare savings, and in increased productivity, which more than make up the difference.

This hot lunch thing really astounds me. Most school lunches absolutely stink. Children are our most valuable resource, and lunch is their most important meal, and now it really is a complete throw away. Real, healthy lunches cost more, and we, as individuals, and entities, have got to spend more time, money, and care on this critical meal. I'm just saying....

I put out a monthly lunch menu, with one option each day, and parents choose which meals they'd like their students to eat and return the menu and payment to me. Copies of these menus are posted on my website (www.realmealsfoodcompany.com). The Waldorf school menus were a bit different from those at the more mainstream school that I'm now at. The more mainstream kids wanted more mainstream food (go figure) so I learned to make typical lunch fare like tacos, cheeseburgers, hot dogs, mac and cheese, grilled cheese and nachos, and make them healthy. I learned that this is possible, that you can feed children chicken fingers and french fries that are actually good for you, or at the very least not bad for you, with no artificial ingredients.

I've looked at quite a few "healthy kids" cookbooks, and as soon as I see the word tofu I put them down. Not to say that offering "health food" to children is at all wrong (although with the preponderance of soy in the typical American diet I'm not sure that tofu even qualifies as health food anymore). I wholeheartedly applaud anyone who feeds their children a diet comprised of organic whole grains and seeds and berries, although I do always counter these people with a story that I once heard about a girl who had been raised in a completely organic environment and lost the ability to walk at age six because she had walked by a lawn that had been recently sprayed (her body was completely unfamiliar with that toxin).

I think you have to go with the flow a little, because this is the world that we live in. I think we can draw the line at certain toxic ingredients, but still allow our children to enjoy a (real) cheeseburger and (real) fries. It is possible to serve a kid friendly, real meal. It's what I do, on a daily basis. It's what this book is about. These recipes are very simple. If they are a springboard to a macrobiotic or raw or vegan diet, cool, because there is no denying that these diets are really, really, healthy. They're just not that feasible for people who enjoy food, of whom I am one. I eat lots of salads and veggies, but I do enjoy a good cookie, and as I sell "Real Cookies" at local farmers markets over the summer and after school on Fridays (a big hit) they're always around. Lucky me.

On the other hand, my daughter, who is now sixteen, helps me at the markets over the summer, and would be perfectly happy to never see another cookie ever again. She doesn't love sweets, which I believe is because of her homemade baby food. Starting children off with real food from the get go and never getting into the blue and orange and red sugary treats will make a world of difference. I wish I had known that when my daughter was little.

In these last eight years I've learned a lot about food. I've witnessed the effects that different kinds of foods have on children. And I've made the food journey myself. I've learned more than I want to know, really, about the state of food in America today. I've learned that all this stuff that is in the food that shouldn't be, all the chemicals and additives and dyes and bleaches, it all has an effect on children. And I've learned that the nutrients that today's food lacks are integral to children's development.

I've learned this firsthand. I've seen children who eat a completely processed diet, and children who eat only organic, real food, and I've seen children in between. I've seen how these children perform in school, how they grow, how they learn, how they interact, and I'm telling you **the kids who eat better perform, learn, interact, and grow better.**

I also know that making the switch from processed to real food isn't like just flipping a switch. It takes a little knowledge, some guts, and some time, especially at first. You will be thankful, as you watch your children prosper, that you gutted up and did this.

I did. At work, and at home, I made the switch, and my daughter and I are much, much healthier now than we were six years ago.

I've seen a lot during this food progression.

I've watched children look at their first hot lunch in horror, especially younger children. Processed foods are bright (bleached, usually) and fluffy and stiff. They look like, well, plastic (go figure.) Real foods aren't always as bright; baked goods are a little browner.

4

It takes a few weeks of looking around and noticing that the big kids are eating, and enjoying, the funny looking stuff for many of the younger kids to warm up to it. (It's not horrifying, by any means, just a little different in appearance than what they're generally used to, and appearance is big with younger children, which is either cause or effect of the big food companies' success. That's another book.)

I've seen children start the year picking at these brown desserts and end the year begging for seconds. I've also watched children dive into the candy their parents tucked into their backpack and not be able to sit still or be quiet for after-lunch line up. I've had children tell me that my broccoli was better than ice cream, and I've had children, and adults, tell me with pride that they never touch a vegetable. I've seen a lot.

There absolutely is a contrast between the children who eat real food and those who don't. (If your child is throwing a tantrum right now because you've stopped to peruse this book, then your child is one of the kids who don't, and you need this book. Seriously.)

Please don't be offended by that statement—you're not a bad parent. I can say this freely because I was once you. I didn't always understand the correlation between processed foods and my child's behavior. I wasn't always committed to the real food movement, though I really thought that I was doing a good job of providing a healthy diet for her. I did make her baby food, and I did not feed her sugar, or so I thought (little did I know that the there was this sugar stuff added to ketchup, and yogurt, and cereal, and sandwich bread….).

And when I came home from work when my daughter was three-and-a-half to her slurping an orange popsicle (my mother, who watched her when I worked, had had enough of the "no sugar" rule and insisted that you cannot keep popsicles from children on hot summer days) our lives changed. My mother, who died of pancreatic cancer at 69, formed a special alliance with Chef Boyardee early in her married life and never looked back. She fell hook, line and sinker into the processed food revolution, was convinced that "low fat" or "fat free" (which was really synthetic chemical imitation food), was the healthy way to go, as did many in her generation. I think people

5

of that generation trust their government more implicitly, and really believe that if the FDA says it's good for you, it's good for you.

Unfortunately, the FDA is a branch of the federal government, which is comprised of legislators who depend on monetary contributions to run the campaigns that keep them in office. Those contributions come from special interest lobbies, and the food industry's lobbies are among the biggest and most powerful in the nation. (The current "food czar" at the FDA is Michael Taylor, a lawyer who was once a Monsanto lobbyist, and has worked on and off for that entity, as well as for the feds, for years. Many FDA commissioners come from the Big Food industry—go figure.)

Both of my parents were hooked on this industry's product, processed foods, and I lost both of them (too soon) to cancer.

My mother watched my daughter for me while I worked, and not long after the popsicle incident she started feeding her processed foods and bright orange and blue stuff. Pretty soon tantrums ensued, which were unlike my daughter, and it took me a little minute to figure out where these erratic mood swings in her were coming from. When I did, I changed the way she ate, and they stopped. She's a healthier, more agreeable, more pleasant person now. She's not perfect, though, and being a teenager, will on occasion succumb to peer pressure and eat crap. I can tell right away when she has, and I have to politely ask her to go away from me. Seriously. Processed foods take a toll on her behavior and attitude almost instantly. This stuff, this processed yuck that we've all been eating has immediate and long-term affects on children. It's not really food. FOOD NOURISHES. THIS STUFF (VERY TEMPORARILY) FILLS.

But, as mentioned, I didn't always know this. The thing is, very, very few of us were actually raised organically, and very, very few of us always knew what was happening to our food. The rest of us had to learn about it, often first hand. My food epiphany came over a bag of stuffing. During my first year at the Waldorf school I had made chicken and stuffing for lunch, and a parent approached me, asking whether I had used commercial stuffing. I had, and she was distraught, and I thought, 'what's the big deal, it's just bread.' The next time I was in the grocery store I picked up a bag and read the long list of unrecognizable ingredients, and I was mystified.

We all start somewhere.

I know that there is some defensiveness when it comes to the subject of healthy eating. You're not a bad parent because you've been feeding your families what you thought was a healthy diet. And you're not a bad person if you've been skeptical of the whole "organic" thing.

The word organic itself is scary to some people. I've had people about to buy the zucchini bread that I sell at the farmers markets shudder and walk away when I mentioned that it was organic. I also know people who insist that organic food "doesn't taste right." I know someone who rejects organics because "the taste is washed out." I had a woman tell me once that she had tried some of the organic food out there, but particularly did not care for organic potatoes, because "they just don't taste the same."

What these people don't get is that the organic version tastes the way it's supposed to taste: it's the root, the real thing. Watered down substitutes are the ones that don't taste right. Processed foods may seem more flavorful because of all the chemical additives that are necessary to make up for the tasteless empty food.

Organic food is just food. It's the real thing, minus the chemicals and additives. I know that in general it's more expensive, which makes it seem elitist, and I know that it can seem intimidating.

If you're afraid of "organic" you are not alone. There's definitely a fear out there of the organic movement, a fear that if you go "organic" you will end up wearing long skirts and have gray hair and sandals and smell like incense and eat tofu and brown rice.

The fear is unfounded. Most real-foodists today are not hippie freaks, and they were not raised on a commune. The revelation that the food we eat is linked to our health comes for everyone at different stages in their life. When I had mine, when I realized that what we were eating was not what we should be eating, I changed the way we ate. I saw marked results. And I became a bit angry.

So be angry, don't be afraid! The real food eaters out there started somewhere, and they're not all tree-hugging granola eaters.

Some, (most, I dare say) are just average joes who are simply interested in providing the best future possible for their children, and have come to the realization that the food that they feed them matters.

Here's why it matters:

The bulk of what the American diet consists of is filler. Corn, wheat and soy are three of this nation's four "cash crops" (cotton being the other). To some extent they always were, as these staples are what grew, in abundance, on our sun swept plains, and for a while the amber waves of wheat nourished a prospering nation. The soil that bore our early crops was nutrient dense, from centuries of composting, basically. Soil depletion is a huge part of the problem with food in America today, and that was not invented by corporate greed. The rest of what happened to our food was.

Soil depletion has been occurring on America's farms since they were established. J.I. Rodale (who actually coined the term 'organic' and was also the founder of publishing giant Rodale Inc. which began publishing "Organic Farming and Gardening Magazine" in 1942, and today publishes many health based periodicals such as "Prevention", "Women's Health" and "Men's Health") was perhaps the original crusader for the organic movement. He began this pursuit after researching what he perceived as a correlation between declining soil health and the health of the American people.

Indeed, soil health has been largely overlooked in food production in America, and it's a huge component in the food crisis. The nutrients that we need to survive, and grow, come from the soil. You can't grow tomatoes in sand for a reason. The soil matters. And when you grow the same crop in the same soil year after year the nutrients that a plant requires get sucked from the soil. If there are no nutrients left in the soil, how do you think nutrients get into the food?

They are added to it, of course. "Enriching" food is Big Food's antidote to the no-nutrient problem. Industrialized agriculture, which began it's monolithic rise in the eighties, is all about reducing food to a paste-like substance and simply adding back some of what was lost in the process.

That's contrary to what farming had always been in this country.

Think about the eighties. Images of farmers will probably shoot through the montage that is conjured in your brain when you reminisce about this era. They were such a part of the social landscape, not for what they'd done, but for what was happening to them. Forces at work before the eighties led to their particular plight, which became damning to our nation's health. A few pivotal occurrences in the seventies set the stage for the perfect storm of corporate greed and perceived necessity that led to our food crisis.

I grew up in the seventies, and I can tell you that when Hamburger Helper came on the market I think my mother saw God. The mothers of this generation were experiencing liberation on many fronts, none as important as in the kitchen. The self worth that these women sought could not be redeemed in the house—they were looking for ways to define themselves that did not incorporate what they cooked. They wanted out of the kitchen, and they dove headfirst into the processed food revolution. This was happening at about the same time that special interest groups were descending like locusts on Washington. The ever-increasing power of these groups brought "corporate-friendly" legislation which allowed for less stringent guidelines and labeling practices.

So, in essence, food companies could fill this growing need for fast, convenient food with watered down versions, producing "imitation" substitutes that no longer had to be labeled such at a fraction of what it cost to produce the real thing. And as we, as a nation, started getting busier and busier, we started caring less and less about what we ate, as long as it was fast. The food companies responded, sometimes jumping over themselves in an effort to think of ways to make meals as quick and convenient as possible. It became a kind of game—"look, Herb, a full turkey dinner in less than 20 minutes!"

Food preparation, once a part of the family ritual, was becoming obsolete. Instead of Mary peeling carrots and Tommy peeling potatoes and Gretchen cleaning up the scraps and setting the table

Mom came home and opened a few bags or boxes. The kitchen, once the heart of the home, became unimportant. Children, teens and dads crept into their own corners, and the de-socialization of America had begun. The slow food movement is about bringing back the kitchen, making it a central part of daily life again, and embracing the meal and meal-making process. I know you think you don't have time for this, but you do, and your teenagers certainly do.

I think so many of the country's ills would be cured if we would again embrace this lifestyle. Think of warm cozy evenings in the kitchen, the whole family involved in the meal preparation process, discussing the day's events, learning moral lessons that they can't get from their XBox. Our kids, especially our teens, though disconnected, are really yearning for this kind of structure, and centering it on food prep is a great way to start bringing them back. In this techno-crazy existence of ours there's something very grounding about preparing meals together.

I know there are some of you who are now picturing (with disdain) families around a wood burning stove singing Kum Ba Ya and churning their own butter, but it doesn't have to be all that. A child of seven should be able to peel a potato. Teens can certainly start meals. Engaging your child in this process makes the process much easier, and I believe that, in general, today's children really need to be brought back to the table, as it were.

So the increasingly busy American family went skipping, hand in hand with the increasingly greedy food companies, into the eighties. Of course the small farmer lay directly in their path (actually, eight million small farmers, of whom six million were wiped out.[1])

Few who were around in the eighties can remove the pictures of farm auctions from their heads. When big business "bought out" the small farmer in this country, things really changed. Our nations declining health is a result of these changes. The route of industrialized agriculture could have been one that cultivated the earth and respected the small farmer and their love of the land, in which American culture had been so rooted. "Big food" could have chosen to spend the money that "doing it right" would have required. They chose instead to pad their pockets.

From Treelight.com: "It is a sad fact that American corporations put profit above all other considerations—above morality, above truth, above our health. They don't regulate themselves, they're not held in check by government, and the fiction that they are regulated by "the market" is, quite simply, a lie."[2]

In this country the dollar reigns supreme, sadly, and when food became big business, i.e. a means for a few people to get really rich, food became a commodity, not food.

When industrialized agriculture took over the small farms crop rotation pretty much went out the proverbial window. It was more economical to only grow cash crops. So instead of a small farm growing multiple crops, and rotating those crops, and thinking about the soil that they were grown in, these companies pursued the route of cash farming, solely developing one of our nation's cash crops, which, as mentioned, depletes the soil.

The other effect of cash-crop farming is bugs. Crop rotation, which is pivotal in organic farming, is necessary for soil development, and is also important in the fight against pests. When you grow the same thing in the same space each year, you get the same kinds of bugs. And if you spray chemicals for those bugs each year, guess what they do? They resist the chemicals, because they want to become stronger bugs. So the bugs actually become bigger and more prevalent, requiring stronger pesticides and scarier chemicals. You can see where I'm going with this.

Organic farmers rotate their crops, and they employ the use of the good bugs that make the bad bugs go away, and they don't use synthetic fertilizers or pesticides.

Pesticides cause cancer (indeed, 45% of all cancers are diet related[3]) and are now being linked to the ADHD that has taken on epidemic proportions in America today.

The organic farmers that I know take soil preparation seriously, because they understand this critical step. This is one of the most compelling arguments for eating organically grown foods. The nutrients that we need to live, to grow, to learn come from the soil, and food that's grown organically lacks chemical pesticides, and is richer in vital nutrients.

Conventional processed food in America today is devoid of vital nutrients. It consists of genetically engineered cash crops (wheat, corn, soy) grown on over-farmed, depleted land, doused with chemicals, "enriched" and prettily packaged. How have they gotten us to eat this stuff?

By making it big and fluffy and bright and beautiful.

Shelf life, appearance, consistency, and, of course, marketability are the catch phrases of the large food manufacturing beasts. These are the components of a successful product. They are what dictate the production of nearly everything on your grocers' shelves. And they have nothing to do with nourishing your child.

Think about the average baked good. It costs about seventy-nine cents. Out of that seventy-nine cents you must pay celebrity endorsers, ad companies, packaging designers, marketing researchers…how much is left to spend on the food?

Organic food costs a bit more simply because it takes more people to produce it (not market it—grow it). It takes human power. It takes farmers who work their soil and control pests without pesticides. Personally I'd prefer my dollar going to the small farmer rather than the celebrity spokesperson. I'm just saying….

Selling a product has become far more important than producing that product. Marketing is yet a different book, but let me just say that it's what food companies spend their money on. If they'd put that money into the food, nurture the soil, rotate their crops, diversify, and strive to use sustainable, pesticide-free growing methods, we would save big dollars in healthcare, and we could once again be the best and brightest and strongest and healthiest nation on earth. We would be so much more if we'd just eat better.

In order for food companies to make enough to pay for marketing and advertising and endorsements and special interest groups and contribute to political campaigns and, oh yeah, get rich themselves, they need to produce food really, really cheaply, utilizing three of our four cash crops (if only they could think of a way to feed us cotton). How?

Start with watered down, genetically modified, over-farmed, toxin-coated, over-processed wheat. Because it has been stripped of the few nutrients it could muster up in these deplorable growing conditions, (to the point that it is basically wheat starch, not flour) it must be "enhanced". The result is this talcum powder stuff that is now know as "enriched flour".

This enriched flour provides a base that is, well, powder, produced very cheaply. How to sell this stuff, en masse, to the masses?

Food producers needed something to combine with all of this wheat-like stuff that would make it fluffy and pretty, and make it last for, oh, say a year or two, on a shelf (think Twinkie).

Baked goods with a shelf life of more than a week or two, at the most, can't be considered real food. (Contrary to urban lore, the Twinkie purportedly has a shelf life of twenty-five days, which, though not the two years that we thought it was, is still a really long life for a food product.) Think about it. Real bread, made with just flour and yeast and salt and sugar, lasts maybe a week.

Hydrogenated oil was their answer. It was created to give baked goods unnatural shelf life (convenient that we had all of this soy around). Adding hydrogen to soybean oil makes this plastic stuff that makes bread fluffy and last for a long, long time. Kind of like play-dough. Yum. Unfortunately our bodies have no idea how to process this plastic stuff. How it actually affected humans was, well, not their concern.

But uh-oh, what about corn? Before hydrogenated oils hit the scene, corn oil was the shortening of choice among food producers. After all, we have all this corn, and it needs to be bought so that Big Food can stay big. Corn is the granddaddy of all cash crops, and Americans consume 1540 pounds of corn per capita each year[4], making us the world's largest corn consumers.

Well, baked goods basically require flour (yeah, wheat) and shortening (yeah, soybean oil) and sugar.

Sugar? But America needs to sell corn.

What if corn could be made into sugar? Wouldn't that be cool? Then food producers could utilize the nation's three big cash crops to produce food that, though absent any nutritional value, could be produced really, really cheaply and take on a vast array of shapes, colors, names and flavors, and they could effectively cram these three cash crops down the throats of unsuspecting citizens. And the really cool thing is, the more we, the citizens, eat of this stuff the more we crave it, the less energy we have, the more inclined we are to, well, sit on the couch and eat more of this stuff, until we're sick, and need to be on constant medication (enter pharmaceutical companies....another book) to deal with what has happened to our bodies from eating too much of this food-like stuff that isn't really food.

So we need sugar, or some kind of sweetener, and we have a lot of corn. Hmmm....

Enter high fructose corn syrup, or the devil, as I affectionately refer to it. This insidious substance, combined with hydrogenated oil and "enriched flour" are what we, our children, and especially our teens, are consuming, thanks in part to the huge marketing apparatus that these food companies rely on.

Hand in hand these substances have destroyed the health and well being of an entire nation. Think about life, and food, before these substances loomed on the food landscape. Think about the great generation—they were the smartest, most decent people, they held the most potential. They were the golden people. We were a golden country. Everyone wanted to be us.

Nobody wants to be us now. We're sick, lazy and tired. The lethargy that has paralyzed this nation is attributable to the food that has been fed to us. The fact is it's just cheaper and easier to eat a mainstream diet.

This is, of course, by design. Did you know that in Michigan there was a movement afoot (and an actual bill that passed the Michigan Legislature) that would allow bridge card (food stamp) recipients to receive their aid twice a month, as opposed to monthly, as had always been the practice? This was done so that aid recipients would be more likely to buy fresh produce. There is also a move in the US congress to disallow this—why? Think about it.

Our decline began when our food changed. I know that this seems like a radical statement to some of you, but seriously, look at what has happened to us, as a people, as a nation, in the last forty years.

One in six children in this country are now diagnosed with a developmental disability[5] (ADHD or autism, mainly).

Diagnosed cases of Autism rose 800% in the nineties[6].

ADHD cases have risen from 150,000 in 1970 to one million in 1985 to 6 million by the year 2000[7]. According to the CDC, 10% of American children have now been diagnosed with the syndrome[8]. There's been a 25% increase in diagnosed cases in the last four years. And two-thirds of these children have been prescribed pharmaceutical medications as a result.

Cancer, once practically unknown in western civilization (and still virtually absent from non-western cultures) now kills one in three people in America. It and heart disease kill nearly 50% of us.[9]

Type II diabetes (again, virtually unheard of prior to the seventies) is now rampant. Experts are now apparently predicting that one in three of today's children will be saddled with this malady.[10]

Type II (adult onset) diabetes is the result of the pancreas, which metabolizes sugar, not processing sugar correctly. High fructose corn syrup is not metabolized by the pancreas, but by the liver, putting unneeded strain on the liver and confusing the pancreas. I am mystified that medical professionals have not drawn the obvious link here. Take away the high fructose corn syrup, and we would begin to see the decline of this disease.

And in addition to all the health risks of this processed yuck that we've been consuming, no one is really talking about what's happening in our schools. Our children are not learning, or performing, at the level that they were fifty years ago. I was speaking with an educator recently who commented that the change in food has been felt nowhere greater than in the classroom, where teachers are met with children who simply cannot focus after 1:00, leaving upwards of two hours for that teacher to try to teach a group of over-stimulated, undernourished children.

Our children are not learning all that they could, and they're falling behind. They were once the smartest on the planet.

American students are not even on the current "smartest top twenty" list.

We're not the best and the brightest anymore.

We could be again, though. We come from good stock. We need to go back to our roots, to our heritage, which has with it an inherent love and respect of the land, and revere the earth again. We once were the land of plenty, and we were healthy. Growing and preparing good food, eating real meals, were once what we were about.

We used to understand agriculture, and the place of farmers in our fabric. When attempting a lifestyle change for your children, this is a really good place to start. Today's kids are really, really disconnected from the food process. When Jamie Oliver began his noble plight and took on school lunches in England I remember him talking about the obstacles he had encountered, and he told a story about celery: he had been trying to engage students in the real food revolution, and had people dress up in vegetable costumes, and the children did not know what the celery was—they'd never seen a piece of fresh celery. They had to be introduced to produce.

Engaging kids in the food process will help you change the way they eat. Understanding this process, from seed to stomach to brain, is important. They need to understand the difference between nourishing and filling, because the food companies don't. They go from (genetically modified) seed to TV commercial to stomach, and don't consider the brain, or other vital organs, like the pancreas. The stuff that they're selling us fills us up, and it tastes good, and it's attractive, and it's durable. It's prepared in a factory. It's not nourishment.

So many people today are missing this point. Full is not nourished. The lunches that I see the mainstream child eat exemplify this: they have bulk, but no 'bang', no power. Because these lunches are fun and pretty and oh-so-sweet (and yes, addicting) they are readily consumed, and kids begin to crave this crap.

And inevitably unhappiness, irritability, meanness, exhaustion, and yes, tantrums ensue. When these tantrums begin, they are irritating, and they are a cry for help. These children's systems are screaming for nourishment.

Children who don't regularly eat this processed stuff often come home from the conventional birthday party with a headache, a glazed-over stare and biting anger. I've seen this, in my house, in the school, at the grocery store. I don't think I've ever seen a well-fed (or well-nourished, I should say) child throw a full-blown tantrum. Seriously.

Until my daughter started displaying this bizarre behavior this tantrum thing was really foreign to me, I have to say.

My sister is a nanny, and before I had my daughter she had a ward that had uncontrollable outbreaks, and I was appalled. Tantrums did not really occur when I was growing up. Only in rare instances did a child behave hysterically. I never threw a tantrum. I couldn't believe the stories my sister told me about this child's frightening behavior, and of course, blamed the parenting (not the nanny, of course). I was certain that no child of mine would ever behave like this.

And then my daughter started displaying these disturbing behavioral patterns, and I couldn't believe it. Tantrums, behavioral issues, and weight gain are all symptoms of malnutrition. Yes, overweight people are often malnourished, meaning that they consume more calories than they need but are not satisfying their nutritional needs.

When my daughter's nutritional needs are not met she becomes angry, mean, unreasonable, hysterical, and sick. I was mortified when, not long after the afore-mentioned popsicle incident, she started throwing these tantrums. It took me a while, but I did begin to suspect that what she ate was affecting her behavior. Then, shortly after my mom had died, while vacationing with relatives at Lake Michigan, there was a specific incident that confirmed my suspicions: we had gone to see a play and wandered into a candy store afterwards. Against my better judgment I let her partake, as all of the cousins were buying little bags of brightly colored sugar stuff. When it was time for bed she became uncontrollable, unable to lay still or quell the meanness that had arisen in her, much to my horror. Here I was with all of my relatives and my little angel had become a monster. I was mortified.

It was like a clinical trial. I saw what that candy had done to her: it made her the devil. I knew then that we needed a food exorcism.

She is sixteen now, in tenth grade, and she gets it.

When she was in middle school (she attended the school that I cook at) she had the privilege of serving as a gym assistant for the kindergarten class on Fridays. After a month, in conversation, she mentioned the names of the kids who were still functioning at 2:30 for gym. Guess what: they were the four children who only ate real food. I swear this is true.

How do you explain that?

Processed food does not provide the fuel that a child needs to get through an average day.

Well, you say, expecting a five year old to perform at 2:30 on a Friday is asking too much.

And I say that's lowering the bar. It's not too much to ask. That child is only halfway through his day. It is a misconception that kids come home whipped from school and can't do anything but sit in front of an electronic screen. My daughter doesn't. She still comes home and heads outside to ride bikes or play. I don't believe that computers and video games are making our children obese. I believe that they are the symptom, not the cause. After exerting themselves physically, intellectually and emotionally for eight hours on an empty nutritional tank, their nutritional needs not being met, they don't have the energy to do anything but sit. That's a really, really big problem.

One of the unique facets of Waldorf education is their approach to homework, which they don't espouse. They believe that a child who has spent eight hours learning needs to spend the next eight stretching (basically, absorbing what they've learned in a free environment, letting their imaginations work, exercising their minds). And while I'm not saying forget about the homework, I am saying that before the homework they need to go play outside for a bit. Kids need exercise, and they need free time.

Really, there are four things that the healthy child needs: food, water, sleep and air, as in fresh air. And if they're properly nourished they will want to go play outside.

And they (desperately) need sleep. Sleep deprivation is epidemic in this country. Our diet has a lot to do with this.

74% of Americans don't get enough sleep each night,[11] and 50% of us can't get out of bed in the morning without an alarm clock.[12] Drowsy driving is the cause of 100,000 accidents each year, resulting in 71,000 injuries and 1500 deaths.[13]

Sleep deprivation, the diminished ability to function properly caused by lack of sleep, leads to stress, anger, and a weakened immune system. 40% of Americans are moderately or severely sleep deprived.[14] This doesn't just mean sleepy or tired, it means deprived to the point that their ability to function normally is compromised. Sleep isn't just resting, anymore than filling is nourishing. We need sleep to repair the damages of the day, to transfer nutrients to vital organs.

Children NEED 9-10 hours of sleep each night. Again, this is a need, not a want. And it should take your child 20-30 minutes to fall asleep at night. If your children are falling asleep the minute their heads hit the pillow they're sleep deprived.

This goes for teens as well. The average teen gets 7 ½ hours of sleep each night, and they require 9 ½. 60% of high school and college students don't get enough sleep,[15] and 30% fall asleep in class at least once a week.[16] Not getting enough sleep can lead to poor grades, ADHD and behavior problems.

It is nearly impossible for children, especially teens, to get the sleep they require, given their crazy schedules. Things like sports, band, drama and debate often require teens to be out until ten or even eleven o'clock. Many high schools start at 7 or 7:30. Obviously this math falls short. I personally believe that middle and high schools should start later, and give props to Robert Bobb of the Detroit School District, who, in his campaign to right the troubled district, actually met with and responded to students, who gave a resounding plea for a later start time.

A person that sleeps 90 minutes less than is needed has their ability to reason diminished by 30%.[17] I don't know about you, but the teens that I know can't afford to lose ANY of their reasoning capacity. They, more than anyone, I dare say, really need the reparation that only sleep can provide.

In order for this reparation to occur the body must be hydrated. Dehydration is also rampant in this country. 75% of Americans suffer from chronic dehydration.[18]

Water is essential to the human system. It regulates body temperature, is necessary for proper circulation, digestion, nutrient absorption and waste elimination. Indeed, 75% of the brain and 70% of muscle tissue are comprised of water.

Dehydration leads to fatigue (if you're yawning in the afternoon, chances are you don't need a nap, you need some water), headaches, and diminished brain function. Often, when feeling thirsty or craving liquid, we grab a soda, which not only doesn't hydrate, but because of its high sodium content, can actually contribute to dehydration.

I wish that all the pop machines in schools could be replaced with purified water systems. Sundance Film Festival adopted this system, using those cool new water bottles, and placing fresh water dispensaries throughout the festival, and in one week saved 50,000 water bottles. Short of that, water bottles should be readily available to students (and recycled responsibly, of course.) They need 64 oz. of water each day. Fresh fruits and vegetables, especially greens, are also hydrating. At the risk of sounding repetitive, this is a NEED. People NEED water.

The optimum goal is for your child to be eating enough of the right kinds of foods, as little as possible of the wrong kinds, getting enough sleep, staying hydrated, and getting a healthy dose of exercise in the FRESH (outside) air. (Inherent in fresh air is sunshine. Humans need sunlight, which provides far more Vitamin D than anything that comes from a cow. Truly. Did you know that rickets has made a comeback here, in America? It has, thanks to the mega doses of sunscreen that are being slathered on our kids, but that's yet another book.)

I maintain that this optimum goal should be the status quo. This is a crazy, crazy world. I don't think we can even fathom the challenges that our children will encounter. In order for a kid to have a fighting chance, they should be starting off healthy. Not just within the parameters of what modern medicine calls healthy, but really, truly healthy. They need real food to achieve that level of "good health."

It's kind of funny (or not) that I'm writing a book about why you should eat real food. My whole premise for this venture (and in life) is that people need real food. Funny that this has become a novelty, or a bent. It was how our great-grandparents lived. In fact, digging out your great-grandmother's cookbooks is a great place to begin. Likewise ingredients: if something wasn't around when your great-grandparents were around it is pretty safe to assume that it's not real and should not be consumed. Jamie Oliver has said that if an item's ingredients sound like a NASA experiment you shouldn't eat it, but if they sound like the ingredients in your nana's pantry, you should.

These next items are the things that you should not consume. They are things used in food processing to produce replicas of real food items at a fraction of the cost. This is what all of this argument boils down to: avoid these things. They aren't in real food. In the good/not bad/bad, spectrum, they are BAD.

Your entire family needs to know about these substances. Engaging your children in the discussion of what high fructose corn syrup is will help you get them off of it. They need to be off of it. It's a horrendous substance that should be banned, and while it's in my top three "don't eats" it's not the first, and when I tell you what that is, I know many of you will shout with anger and horror and some of you may throw the book down and stomp on it, but it has to be said.

*   *   *   *   *   *   *   *   *

The List:

1) Caffeine

Yes, caffeine. It's an extremely harmful drug. I know you think you need it, but you don't.

90% of Americans consume caffeine on a regular basis.[19] No surprise that America's most popular drug is an addictive one. It's a psychoactive stimulant, and it affects the same brain channels as cocaine and amphetamines. It also increases adrenaline production, leaving a person feeling tired and depressed when the adrenaline wears off. So, of course, being tired and depressed, that person will reach for the needed "pick me up", and then they're "up" again. Follow the bouncing ball…..sound familiar?

Caffeine's half-life is six hours, meaning that if you drink a cup of coffee at 3:00, half of the caffeine (50mg) is still in your system six hours later, when you should be winding down. Caffeine consumption leads to sleep deprivation, because the body can't achieve deep, reparative sleep with this amphetamine coursing through its veins. And without that deep sleep a person wakes up tired (humans should wake up feeling refreshed and ready to face the day) and reaches for a morning jolt. And the beat goes on.

Deep sleep (and enough of it) is especially important for children, because growth hormones are secreted at night, so if a child does not get a full night's sleep, their growth will be stunted. Chemicals important to the immune system are also secreted during deep, reparative sleep. Caffeine inhibits these functions. It is also a diuretic, meaning it makes you pee more.

There is no specific number that the FDA recommends in terms of how much caffeine a person should consume (wonder why). It is simply recommended that it be used "in moderation". It actually can be fatal: 3200 mg or more (about 2 gallons of coffee) over a short period of time can kill you. Consuming more than 350mg/day leads to physical dependence on the drug. Here's the rundown on how much is in your favorite beverages:

8 oz coffee—100 mg
8 oz black tea—50 mg
8 oz chocolate milk—48mg
12 oz soda—50 mg
8 oz Red Bull—80 mg.

I know that many of you feel that you can't live without this drug, (and it really is that, an addictive drug) but truly, you can, and you will be SO much more rested, healthy, and happy without it. If you refuse to give it up, at the very least recognize how harmful it is and keep it OUT of your children's diets.

Understand, also, that breaking the habit is not like throwing out an old pair of socks. Withdrawal symptoms can be pretty severe, beginning with splitting headaches. I experienced excruciating pain for seven days when I quit (ibuprofen definitely helped) but I went cold turkey. It was worth it, because I have so much more energy now.

2) High fructose corn syrup

Although there is not yet hard, concrete proof that high fructose corn syrup leads to type-II diabetes, the facts surrounding the disease, and the nearly identical growth timelines of type II diabetes and high fructose corn syrup consumption, really present a strong argument, I think.

High fructose corn syrup is not metabolized by the pancreas, (whose main job in life is to metabolize sugar), but by the liver, (whose job it isn't).

The liver has a hard time processing (or even recognizing) this stuff, so it cannot process it rapidly. The excess is stored as fat, and fat in the liver leads to insulin resistance, which is what type-two diabetes really is.

Don't be fooled by those commercials, high fructose corn syrup is not the same as sugar. It has practically the same glycemic index as sugar, but it is not the same.

Here's the thing about sugar: a little is fine, even necessary. The USDA recommends that a 2000-calorie diet should contain 8 teaspoons of sugar (in any of its many forms) each day. That's almost a quarter of a cup.

One 12oz can of Pepsi contains just over 8 teaspoons of high fructose corn syrup, 103% of the daily requirement. And remember, this stuff is in everything, from cereal to bread to yogurt to juice to ketchup. So if you drink three sodas and eat conventional, processed foods all day, you are consuming upwards of 500% of the recommended amount of sweetener each day. The human body is just not equipped for that kind of overload.

Cutting out pop is really a huge step when trying to right the way your family eats. Conventional soda pop is nothing more than wasted calories. It's not even hydrating. There is absolutely nothing redeeming about it.

My daughter and I will, on occasion, get a six-pack of pop (made with cane sugar) from Whole Foods for the weekend and split it. Make it a special occasion thing, or learn to make your own. Soda should never be looked to as a staple. Seriously.

High fructose corn syrup was actually invented as a means of selling corn. Adding enzymes to corn that's been soaked in sulfur dioxide and wet-milled makes this goo that your body really doesn't recognize or know what to do with. Since the genetically modified, highly-pesticided, over-farmed corn that now sweeps our amber plains is pretty much absent any nutrients, turning it into a goop that adds a sticky sweetness to EVERYTHING seems like, well, good business. Never mind the health implications.

The average American consumes 41.5 pounds of this stuff each year.[20]

There's no question that the epidemic of obesity and the dramatic rise of ADHD, autism, cancer and diabetes in this country began when our food changed. High fructose corn syrup, hydrogenated oils and enriched flour are really the big three in this new American cuisine of ours.

High fructose corn syrup adds large amounts of a non-food substance to your system, putting severe strain on your liver and pancreas. It causes dramatic behavior issues and mood swings. It provides short bursts of (often frenetic) energy followed by severe slumps that make a person feel tired and depressed. Some studies also link it to the suppression of leptin, the hormone that makes you feel full, which leads to overeating (you eat, you don't feel full, you eat some more, and some more, and.....)

We consume so much more stuff than we need to here in America because the crap we're eating isn't fulfilling our nutritional needs.

This crap is just filler, sort of loosely based on what was once real food, altered and stripped and regurgitated into pretty, sweet nothings. The homo sapien existed for 200,000 years on this earth eating real food, and in the last fifty years, since the advent of food processing to this extreme, we've seen a marked transformation. Our new synthetic diet is leading to the creation of a new, fatter, meaner, dumber version of the human being, the homo sloth, if you will.

The fact that there is no hard data linking high fructose corn syrup to obesity, diabetes, heart disease and ADHD doesn't say as much about its actual health risks as it does about the power of the corn industry's lobby. It's nasty stuff. Take your family off of it, and you will see a tangible change in your children.

3) Hydrogenated Oils

The American obesity epidemic began when coconut oil (then the fat of choice for baking) was replaced by partially hydrogenated soybean oil. From the Treelight Website: "Trans fats are poisons, just like arsenic or cyanide. They interfere with the metabolic process of life by taking the place of a natural substance that performs a critical job. And that is the *definition* of a poison. Your body has no defense against them..."[21]

Enough said?

Hydrogenated oils interfere with the body's ability to process good fats, which are an essential component of the human diet. They are largely comprised of soybean oil, which suppresses the thyroid, lowering energy levels. Adding hydrogen to soybean oil makes it into a more stable substance, kind of like plastic or rubber, thus dramatically increasing the shelf life of food. It also makes the texture of food more palatable and the food prettier—less greasy, fluffier, stiffer, as if something like...well, plastic, had been added to the food.

This synthetic stuff is really dangerous, and is not used much outside of the U.S. except by countries that are involved with

American corporations, who, of course, have been using it with abandon, as it allows them to produce food really cheaply.

Both hydrogenated oils and high fructose corn syrup are pretty much uniquely American.

Just about everyone is now on to the trans fat problem, and it is thankfully starting to be eliminated (NYC, Philadelphia and Boston have now banned the substance). Avoid it at all costs.

4) Enriched flour

Remember when you were in kindergarten at craft time and the teacher pulled out that big jar of paste? For those of you not quite as ancient as myself, back in the day, when Elmer's wasn't a staple but a luxury, schools used these large jars of generic white paste (I'm trying to think of an analogous texture but I can't). That's what I envision when I see the words "enriched flour."

Enriched flour begins with genetically modified, badly over-farmed wheat, really at the far end of what I'd even call real wheat. It is stripped of virtually all of its vitamins and minerals, leaving a very fine-textured substance that is, in essence, wheat starch. Because it is more a starch, which acts like sugar in the body, than a fiber, which is what real flour strives to be, it is absorbed differently. Whole grains are absorbed slowly by the body, providing a static level of energy over an extended period of time (which is why I insist that my daughter eat oatmeal or some kind of whole grain cereal for breakfast). Wheat starch provides the same kinds of intense energy bursts brought on by high fructose corn syrup consumption. So our kids get a big burst of energy right from the get-go, thanks to the cereal that they've just slurped down, and they crash at snack time, grab some crappy snack, then another burst, crash, lunch, spike, crash.....what a day.

It's no wonder our kids are whipped when they get home from school (and no wonder educators will tell you that it is now impossible to actually teach after 1:00 or so). The excess from these bursts of calories into the bloodstream are stored as fat, which the body must then work twice as hard to burn off. The overtaxed system, dealing with these sugar spikes, besides having to fight an uphill battle just to get through the day, soon becomes burdened with type-II diabetes.

So even the most nutritious sounding muffin comprised of enriched flour is really a whole lot of nothing. Because all of the nutrients were stripped out of the wheat, food companies "add" them back, thus "enriching" them, which basically means adding chemical derivatives of the nutrients that were actually there, but removed.

From globalhealingcenter.com: "Carbs should come from unrefined sources, like fresh organic fruits and vegetables. Not from something that's been processed and bleached and then had trace amounts of synthetic nutrients added back in so that the "industry" can sleep at night."[22]

Now, keep in mind that organic white flour is still highly processed. White flour really is just paste (remember your early paper-mache projects?). Organic white flour, however, is not genetically altered, and is not "enriched" so nothing synthetic is added. And it is not bleached. If a little white flour gets your child to eat some oats and whole grains and nuts and fruit, like in banana bread, for instance, I say okay, as long as it's organic. Flour is a means to an end, though, and should not be looked to as a nutrition staple.

The thing is, that piece of banana bread, made with organic white and wheat flour, oats, and nuts, is sating. We can afford to eat some delicious, organic, homemade baked goods, because they're eaten in moderation—you don't want or need to eat a whole bag of "Real Cookies" in one sitting—one will actually fill you up and provide static energy so you're not hungry again in an hour, unlike their highly-processed store-bought counterparts. And because a "Real Cookie" is not introducing any synthetic substances to confuse and overwork your system your body is free to perform all of its essential functions to utmost capacity. The human body is an amazing thing. Just treat it right and it will last you a lifetime.

On the subject of treating your body right, the remaining eight items on my dirty dozen list are all man-made substances added to the food we eat to make it more aesthetically pleasing or in some way cheaper to produce. Where that "savings" goes (fat food companies) is yet another book.

The meteoric growth of the chemical industry after World War II inevitably affected the food industry, and subsequently our health, in profound ways. These additives are the products of that industry's efforts.

5) MSG

MSG is in everything. Because of FDA labeling criteria it does not have to be listed with an item's ingredients. When it is, it is called many things—sodium glutamate, hydrolyzed vegetable protein, vegetable flavoring, modified food starch, textured vegetable protein, and natural flavoring are a few examples.

Did you know that MSG is actually responsible for creating a race of rodents? Scientists who needed obese mice and rats for diabetes testing created this race of uber-rodents by injecting them with…you guessed it…MSG. MSG triples the amount of insulin produced by the pancreas of rats.

Does it do that to humans? Have there even been any tests performed?

John Erb, who penned The Slow Poisoning of America, claims that it is added to food because of its addictive effect. It was first introduced in the sixties, and the FDA does not limit how much of it food companies can add to our food.

MSG, or monosodium glutamate, is an excitatory neuro-transmitter, or excitotoxin, which is a substance that can cause sensitive neurons to die. It was originally produced from seaweed, but is now created from genetically modified bacteria. It actually stimulates the taste buds, then the brain, making food "taste better."

MSG has been linked to obesity, diabetes, migraines, headaches, autism, ADHD and Alzheimer's.

It has actually spurred some legislation, though. Have you ever heard of the cheeseburger bill? This is legislation that was introduced by George W., passed by the House in 2004, rejected by the Senate, then reintroduced in 2005 by Florida Congressman Ric Keller, whose PAC accepted the maximum dollar amount in donations, (pre-"Citizens United") from fast food companies. This law would make it impossible to sue any food companies for health issues brought on by the food that a person has consumed. Officially called the "Personal Responsibility in Food Consumption" act, what this legislation is proposing, in essence, is that Big Food can feed us anything they want, and if it makes us sick, or obese, or it kills us, we have no legal recourse. It's good to see our tax dollars working so hard for us, isn't it?

The Minnesota House of Representatives passed their own Cheeseburger Bill in 2011, but it was (thankfully) vetoed by that state's governor.

6) Aspartame

Also an excitotoxin, this artificial sweetener has been linked to the high incidence of cancer among Desert Storm soldiers because it turns to methanol when heated past 86 degrees, which then becomes formaldehyde. The FDA limits methanol intake to 7.8 mg/day, while one liter of diet soda contains 56 mg. And unless you know that your diet soda is being shipped in refrigerated trucks, you're drinking formaldehyde, which is a know carcinogen that can cause birth defects and brain tumors.

If you need more reasons to eliminate it from your diet, it kills neurons in the brain, and has been linked to headaches/migraines, abdominal pain, fatigue, sleep problems, vision problems, anxiety, depression, joint pain, and can disrupt your menstrual cycle.

The blood brain barrier, which normally protects the brain from excess glutamate and aspartate, is not fully developed in children, making it even more dangerous for them to consume.

It's really just in diet pop, which is just useless chemical crap, and if you only take one thing away from this book, let it be that KIDS

DON'T NEED SODA POP. It's in some lemonades and sparkling waters too, so read your labels.

7) Genetically Modified Organisms (GMO's)

You can scrutinize all the labels on grocery shelves and you won't find any that say anything about GMO's, and it's not because they're not there. The Grocery Manufacturers of America estimate that 75% of all the processed food in America contains at least one ingredient that has been genetically altered.[23] Even though the European Union, Japan and Australia require genetically modified food items to be labeled as such, the US and Canada don't require any kind of labeling at all. In fact, there are no specific safety tests required by the FDA for GMOs---go figure. And in the US today, 93% of all soybeans, 86% of corn, 93% of cotton, 13% of zucchini, and until a recent lawsuit brought by the Center for Food Safety halted its production, 95% of sugar beets, are all genetically modified. We better hope there's nothing harmful in them, since they're obviously everywhere.

A GMO is a genetically modified organism. Genetic engineering, the transferring of specific genes, or traits, from one organism to another, hit the food scene in the mid '90s. Led by Monsanto (more on them later,) the industry went crazy with this, as it was yet one more way to increase profits via chemically altering the food. Although there have been some genetic modifications that produce certain characteristics in produce (the Flavrsavr Tomato) genetic modification's primary use has been in bug control—food gurus thought that they could breed plants that were "naturally" resistant to pesticides. Their plan has kind of backfired, as more and more chemicals are being required to kill the super weeds that these GMO's are also creating. The weed resistance brought on by increased GMO use led to an actual increase (70 million pounds worth) in U.S. pesticide use from 1996-2003.

Just like with MSG, the fact that there is no evidence linking GMO's to any health issues does not mean they're not there, just that there has not been adequate (any) testing. Like with the growth hormones you're about to read about, Monsanto says they're safe, so that is pretty much the final word. Why would Monsanto lie to us? Hmmmm....

The camps that are opposed to GMO's cite the alarming rise of food allergies in children as one of the side affects of genetically altering a plant, as introducing a new gene into a plant may create new allergens. When a gene is mutated, the mutating substance must have a host, which is either bacteria or virus, and many scientists are concerned about the ramifications of introducing a new bacteria or virus into genes—concerned not because they've found hard evidence proving the harm in this, but because there just has not been enough time, or testing, done. It's virtually unheard of for something with so many questions surrounding it to be introduced into the market on this wide a scale, isn't it?

Why is it being allowed? Hmmmm.....

8) Hormones, steroids and antibiotics

These are lumped in together because they are used pretty much interchangeably.

In an effort to increase milk production, food producers began using synthetic hormones and/or steroids (and by using I mean injecting livestock with) in the early nineties. Prior to that the average dairy cow produced 5300# milk/year. Today that cow produces 18,000 pounds annually.[24] 80% of American cows are injected with artificial growth stimulators.[25]

The granddaddy of synthetic growth substances is the genetically engineered bovine growth hormone, known as rBGH, BGH, BST or rBST. You'll never guess who makes it. Until very recently Monsanto owned the patents on this stuff, and they stood to lose billions if it were banned in America, as it has been pretty much everywhere else in the world. The United Nations Food Safety Agency, which represents 101 nations worldwide, voted

31

unanimously in favor of supporting the 1993 European moratorium on rBGH. Yes, American milk is banned in Europe and Canada.

Why is this? Supporters of using genetically-engineered synthetic chemicals to increase milk production argue that there is not enough evidence linking these additives to any serious maladies to warrant its removal from the food production process. Just like with MSG, that's because there's really been very little testing done.

To the best of my knowledge, milk producers are not required to list rBGH on food labels, and you'll actually see it more on labels stating that it's not being used (many labels will say "No rBGH").

And though you do see the "No rBGH" label on milk more and more now, you rarely see it on butter or cheese, or on ground beef, and unless the product specifically says "No growth hormones, steroids, or antibiotics," it's a pretty safe bet that the said product is simply not safe to eat (the organic label, of course, will suffice, as all of these substances are absolutely forbidden in organic food production.)

One article that I recently read said that this stuff is like crack for cows. It makes the animals really sick. The increased milk production makes the strung-out cow develop mastitis (sores on the udders) and require a steady stream of antibiotics. Antibiotics and growth promoters are a package deal, and all this antibiotic is really not good for humans, who are developing antibiotic resistance and stomach issues (the increased level of antibiotics in our systems actually kills the "good" bacteria required in proper digestion) at an alarming rate. The pandemic of early puberty in girls is largely attributed to this stuff, as is, oh yeah, cancer…breast cancer in particular.

The U.S. Court of Appeals recently upheld a ruling by the 6th Circuit Court in Ohio which ruled that there is a "compositional difference" between treated and untreated milk, those differences being:

a) increased levels of the cancer causing hormone IGF, which is produced by cows in response to BGH injections

b) lower nutritional quality

c) more pus—can you believe this? A glass of conventional, BGH treated milk contains up to 20% pus, which causes milk to sour more rapidly (which is why organic milk lasts so much longer.)

The European union has also banned American beef, 40% of which comes from the sick dairy cows that are no longer able to produce milk with Herculean prowess. The U.S. allows food producers to inject cattle and sheep with synthetic growth promoter, but not chickens, ducks, or turkeys. Unfortunately, eating and drinking only organic dairy and meat does not exempt us from ingesting this stuff, as it is slowly making its way into the ground water, and thus the ecosystem, via cow manure (can't anyone figure out a way to make these cows stop pooing?)

This stuff really should be banned. (It may be banned soon. The fact that Monsanto just dumped this branch is very telling I think).

9) Preservatives

Also really-should-be-banned.

Back in the day, I worked at an upscale steak house, and I'd ask friends to bring me fast food to eat during my break every once in awhile (we didn't serve french fries). When asked why I'd quip that I needed my daily serving of preservatives, as I believed that they were behind our increasing life spans ("they're actually preserving US"). Funny then, not so much now. These substances aren't preserving us, they're making us sick. They're preserving the food, and, you know, increasing the shelf life, etc....

Here's a rundown of some of the more popular preservatives and their related maladies:

Sodium nitrate--causes cancer

Propyl gallate (used to keep fats and oils from going rancid)--headache, joint pain, cancer

Potassium bromate (banned everywhere but in US and Japan)--cancer

Benzoates/sodium benzoate/benzoic acid (banned in Russia)--asthma, allergies, brain damage, behavior issues

Butylates--high blood pressure, kidney and liver malfunction

BHT, BHA--liver disease, cancer

Bromates--nutrient destruction, diabetes

Glutamates--headache and cancer

Mono and diglycerides--birth defects and cancer

We don't need to chemically preserve our food. You don't need to be eating something that's been on your grocer's shelf for weeks, or even months.

Honestly, I'm sure there are more that I've not listed, and I don't pretend to be a scientist or understand the actual mechanics of all of this stuff. I just see what it does to kids, what it's doing to us as a nation, and I know that it needs to be avoided. I don't read all of the big words on the bread labels—if it has more words than flour, yeast, salt, sugar and some kind of shortening, I just put it back.

10) Nitrates

These are preservatives, but they get their own category because they're particularly harmful. And it's not actually the nitrate that is harmful, it's the nitrosamine that it becomes that is a powerful cancer-causing chemical. Nitrates are in some veggies, like spinach, lettuce, celery and green beans, but these foods also contain high levels of vitamins C and D, which actually block carcinogens from forming. Nitrates are used in cured meats, bacon, and hot dogs. A child that eats more than 12 hot dogs/month has 9x the normal risk of developing leukemia. One article that I read suggested that if your child is going to eat a conventional hot dog they should at least drink some OJ with it, so they get the needed vitamin C. My daughter's never really been a fan of the dog, so it was never really an issue for me as a parent. I do serve a healthy version once a month at school (Trader Joe's all beef/all natural/no nitrate hot dogs) and the kids really like them.

11) Artificial colors

According to the FDA, in 1955 Americans ingested 12 mg of food dye per capita, and in 2007 that number had increased to 59 mg. That's an almost 400% increase in the amount of synthetic color we consume. Prior to the 1950s food dyes were mostly made from food products (saffron, carrots, pomegranates, spinach, parsley and beets had all once been used as food colorings). Now, of course, they're petroleum-based, and entirely synthetic. These chemicals are being linked to hyperactivity, asthma, anxiety, depression, migraines, ADHD and cancers of the brain, thyroid and kidneys.

The food industry has known for years that there was a connection between food colors and behavior issues. Now we do. They're completely unnecessary. If you've made the commitment to eschew high fructose corn syrup, hydrogenated oils and enriched flour, ridding your diet of this stuff will not be difficult, as it's simply not used in organic or all natural food (yes, some organic cereals have some colors to them, but they're food based colors, just like in the good old days).

12) Pesticides

If you're eating any genetically modified processed foods you're eating pesticide, so just eating organic produce doesn't necessarily remove the stuff from your diet altogether, but it's a great start. Pesticides are used with abandon here in the US. Atrazene, a pesticide that disrupts hormone production, and is banned in Europe, is apparently in 94% of the water in America. Yuck. The U.S. uses 900 million pounds of pesticide annually.[26] That's roughly three pounds of pesticide/person. Go pick up a 3# jug of Round Up and imagine feeding that to your toddler. Again, yuck. Children are absolutely more sensitive to the effects of this stuff, and the average American kid consumes 5 servings of pesticide residue each day.

Pesticides have long been linked to birth defects, nerve damage and cancer, and a new Harvard study has now linked them to ADHD, which could very well account for that syndrome's unprecedented rise over the last three decades.

The most heavily sprayed items are strawberries, peaches, celery, apples, blueberries, lettuce and spinach. Things like watermelon, pineapple and bananas, which have skins that you don't eat, are safer to eat than a strawberry that's been doused with the stuff. I try to eat as much organic as possible, especially anything that doesn't have a removable outer layer, but some things are just really hard to find. Green beans are a good example. They're one of the veggies that most kids will eat, and because it's almost impossible to find organic green beans, I still serve the conventional ones. I wash them really well, and I figure that in this instance the benefits outweigh the harm. We need fruits and veggies, and if organic is not always an option, then pick and choose: start eliminating the most harmful conventional items, like strawberries.

*   *   *   *   *   *   *   *

These twelve things are what have lead to the health crisis in America. They are the culprits behind imitation food and its production. They are toxins that the human body doesn't know how to process, and they interfere with the ability of vital organs to function properly. They lead to cancer, heart disease, diabetes, depression, ADHD and autism. They mess your body up.

Just eliminate these twelve things.

*   *   *   *   *   *   *

Sounds simple, right? On one level it is, really. Just say no. If you can't pronounce it then don't eat it. The goal, in essence, is to simplify your child's diet by sticking to real food. Dr. Phil says that you should stick to foods that have one ingredient. (He also says that if you're out of breath after reading the ingredients, you shouldn't eat that item.)

If you eliminate these twelve ingredients you will be giving your children the tools they need to achieve their potential. The rest will follow. They'll get enough sleep and they'll be hydrated and they'll come home from school with bright eyes eager to begin the next part of their day. And they'll be productive, and they'll be healthy and they'll be smart and they'll grow up and save the world and there will be peace on earth.

It all starts with the food, and real food is the answer. If we all just ate real food, avoided these twelve things, drank enough water and got enough sleep, health care in this country would be an entirely different beast.

Okay, so all you need to do is avoid these twelve substances, right? Pretty much. And what should they be eating?

If you haven't gotten by now that the obvious answer to the "what should we be feeding our children" question is "real food" you haven't been following along. They need real food.

If you are not already reading the labels of everything you buy in the grocery store, you need to start. When you do, you'll discover why the task of only feeding your families real food requires Olympian dedication. Pretty much everything on your conventional grocers' shelves is imitation.

If you have the financial resources to afford a 30% hike in your family's food costs, making the switch can be pretty simple. Organic grocers, like Whole Foods and Trader Joe's, carry a huge array of "processed" organic fare, much of which is pricey. Though I still recommend cooking as much from scratch as possible, not everyone has the time, and sometimes a can of pasta and toast makes a meal. If it's not a can of organic pasta, it contains a good few of these toxic elements that we are trying to avoid. Eat as much organic as you can afford. It's definitely worth the extra money. There are quite a few organic versions of Spaghetti-O's out there.

While what to feed your family is clearly the paramount topic here, when to feed them merits discussion as well.

WHEN kids eat is important. Remember, the goal is to enable their bodies to work the way that they are supposed to. Really, children should be eating five or six meals each day. Yes, five or six. Pretty much everyone agrees that sticking to three meals doesn't make sense.

The food day should be divided into breakfast, mid-morning snack, lunch, afternoon snack, dinner, and for older children, a light evening snack.

Starting the day out right is clearly important, and sadly overlooked. The rush of the morning has given way to quick-fix, highly processed breakfasts. Toaster pastries and colorful cereals that contain high fructose corn syrup, hydrogenated oils, dyes and additives, are attractive and sweet, but they don't contain any of the nutrients that are needed to rev the proverbial engine. That said, if cereal is a staple, a few simple changes can make a drastic difference. Organic really matters here. An organic cereal comprised of whole grains (and hopefully some nuts and/or fruit), organic dairy or yogurt, and a cup of orange juice (preferably organic, at least American-grown and definitely 100% juice) is a really good start, and will help keep your child's energy level stay static throughout the day.

Of course you can't beat a bowl of oatmeal to rev that engine. Our hard working ancestors knew this. My nanny sister tries to make sure that her wards start the day with oatmeal so that they can make it to the next snack or meal with no whining.

I've never been one to start with a "breakfast" myself. I usually eat a banana and grab some OJ and a handful of granola, but my daughter likes to sit and eat a meal. I think this is good practice, and if you have the time on one or two days, it's nice for your family to be able to share a good meal and compare notes for the day ahead. And really, children deserve a plate of warm pancakes on a snowy morning every once in awhile. Being present at breakfast time and making sure they're getting a good start are small but oh-so-important steps in righting the way your family eats.

The mid morning snack is important as well. Pretty much every school acknowledges this and allows for morning snack. Take advantage of this, especially if you don't have anyone like….well, me…. preparing your child's school lunch, which, by the way, is not that difficult, and should be attempted by a few moms at each school. Seriously. You don't need a factory feeding your child. This is truly a noble pursuit, providing healthy, "Real Meals" for school children each day, and if anyone out there wants to give it a go I'd be more than happy to provide whatever support I can. As a group, we simply must demand more, and as individuals, we really need to do more.

Lunch is arguably the most important meal of the day, and we all now know that the state of public school lunches in this country is abysmal. Children who start the day with processed cereal and chemical laden milk, snack on a "healthy" (have you read the labels?) granola bar or yogurt, and eat a conventional school lunch, have eaten tons of crap but nothing at all nutritious. By the time they get home from school they've worked a full day with no gasoline, just kool-aid in the engine. And we wonder why all they want to do is stare vacuously at an electronic device.

Kids are hungry when they get home from school. If they continue to consume empty calories they will just eat and eat, because this food that is not really food does not sate the body.

Indeed, in the case of high fructose corn syrup, it doesn't even trigger the body's fullness signals. They end up eating lots of empty calories, but they've not been nourished. They're still hungry, and on the road to obesity, heart disease and diabetes. This is sickening.

Since you are sending morning snack and lunch, when they get home from school they will really benefit from some kind of homemade snack. Think of warm apple crisp on a fall afternoon, or warm breadsticks and marinara sauce on a rainy Monday. Walking into a home that smells of freshly baked bread can actually put a smile on a hormonal teenager's face—need I say more?

And don't worry that it will ruin dinner. Dinner should not be the day's biggest meal. I know that you feel like it's the meal that you've put the most work into and it should be eaten. Nibbled at, and eaten tomorrow for lunch, is really just as validating, and much healthier for your child. And it can, and should, still be the most important meal from a social standpoint. I wholeheartedly support the evening meal campaign, as it really is a waning but critical part of our social fabric.

A light dinner of poultry and salad with a whole grain roll or cracker is always a quick option. Stuffing people at 6 PM overtaxes the system, which needs to be focused on the nightly reparation that lies ahead.

An evening snack of dairy or complex carbs, like toast, oats or quinoa (my daughter eats hers with a little cinnamon) to fuel the evening rejuvenation can be a good way to end the food day. There is some research that indicates that milk can promote a restful sleep, but if your child has a hard time processing dairy, or is prone to sinus issues, better skip it. I know it sounds weird, but a baked potato can be a good evening snack. Stay away from sweets, and certainly do not allow chocolate or caffeine. At this point you want to promote a restful night and a good morning, and complex carbohydrates provide hours of sustained energy.

Feeding a child real food throughout the day and keeping them hydrated is what their bodies need. If you are not inhibiting the body in any way, by adding stuff that it doesn't recognize or know how to process, and letting the body work the way it's supposed to, guess what? It will, by and large, work the way it's supposed to, and healthy habits will begin to form on their own.

Listen to cravings. Their bodies are speaking to you. I don't eat meat, but my daughter does, sporadically. When she wants steak I make it for her, because I know she's craving iron. A healthy child will tell you what they need. They'll tell you how much sleep they need as well. My daughter will forego social activities and nap on the couch when she needs to. It takes a little minute to get them off the junk food wheel, but once they are off it they will cooperate, unknowingly perhaps. Let the body work the way it's supposed to, and it will work the way it's supposed to.

A diet consisting of whole grains, leafy greens, and fresh fruits and vegetables is really the healthiest. Of course, there's more to life than granola and brown rice, but you should really try to make whole grains and fresh produce staples. Feed them whole grains, fruits, nuts and veggies whenever possible. They need these things. Each day. These things don't need to be presented in the form of an elaborate dish—a handful of nuts can be incorporated into pretty much anything, from salad to pancakes, and a little goes a long way. A few pieces of raw broccoli with lunch satisfy a veggie requirement.

And you should recognize that children's eating habits begin to change drastically in about the fifth grade. This is when the real physical growth and hormonal changes start kicking in, and those require carbohydrates. Children who are eating a preponderance of carbs before this age are almost always headed for obesity, but pre-teens and teens obviously need them, so make sure they're good carbs, or at the very minimum, not bad ones. They don't need empty filler calories, which is what the bulk of the average teenager's diet consists of, and they certainly don't need toxins or artificial additives. This is a crucial growth period, and they really, really need real food now more than ever. And while I don't advocate drinking milk each day, some teens, boys especially, do tend to grow very fast, and really do need as much calcium as possible. And truly, getting a teenage boy to eat leafy greens or yogurt, is, well, let's just say that they would be a bit more disputed than, say, a glass of cold milk with a warm brownie.

Before we delve into the specifics of what, exactly, you should be feeding your family, we should probably talk about where to get the things you should be eating.

In my neck of the woods Whole foods and Trader Joe's are where the real-foodists predominately shop. These stores offer an extensive array of organic items. Trader Joe's is smaller, in part because they carry very few items that aren't the Trader Joe's brand (saving lots of shelf space and allowing for lower prices). They are less expensive than Whole Foods on many items, but they don't offer quite the selection that Whole Foods does.

I absolutely love my Trader Joe's. It really exudes a 'home-town' grocery feel, it's small, the team members are really friendly and knowledgeable, and when I leave Trader Joe's I really feel like I've gotten the most out of my dollars.

I love my Whole Foods, too. Whole Foods truly is America's organic grocer. In addition to the vast selection of organic foods and beverages that fills their shelves you'll find a huge selection of cleaning products, pet supplies, personal care products and even clothing.

If you choose to live an organic lifestyle, these stores will likely become mainstays.

I am lucky enough to live and work in an area in which both of these stores are located right across the street from each other, which is awesome. These stores often serve as meeting places as well...I rarely get through either of them without running into some old friend that I haven't seen in ages. The real food movement is thriving in both of these venues, and they will become pivotal stops on your journey towards a healthier lifestyle.

In Michigan we are lucky enough to have Meijer as well. Meijer is a chain of superstores, much like Kmart or Walmart, with a much more extensive grocery section.

The Meijer family has made a commitment to organic, to the extent that they carry their own organic line which offers pretty much everything, from pasta, cereal and snack products to dairy, juices, salsa, vegetables and frozen foods. Each Meijer is different, but most carry some organic produce, and many carry quite a bit.

They can be hit or miss, but they do get most of their produce locally, and when items like organic strawberries are in season Meijer is hands down the best place to shop.

Here in Southeast Michigan we also have a company called "Organic by the Case" that offers a good selection of organic foods. Companies like this are popping up everywhere, and technology makes them easy to find.

Many real-foodists also belong to food co-ops. I belong to a United Foods co-op, and I also order from Country Life, which is a Michigan company.

United Foods offers an extensive selection of organic and all-natural items, but I don't think they're accepting new co-ops. You could try to hook up with an existing one. There are many food groups and co-ops out there, and they're not hard to find. If you're unsuccessful finding them online, try networking at your local organic grocery store.

Of course, most, if not all, grocery stores and "warehouse" outlets, like Costco, carry some organic. The larger chains are beginning to see the future, I think, and are starting their own line of organic foods.

Here in America, where capitalism is king, the law of supply and demand is paramount, i.e., if we all stop eating the crap that Big Food is trying to feed us, and ask (quite literally, ASK) for real, organic food, your grocer will start offering a greater selection of healthier options.

Remember, the dollar rules. I have long maintained that we can't blame McDonalds (not wholly, anyways) for this food crisis that we're in. They have merely been responding to consumer demand. Demand better, and watch what happens. We'll start seeing McFruities or McRealFood chains popping up.

Of course, Big Food could follow suit. If they would acknowledge the harm that their product is bringing us and spend the big money that they've been spending on lobbying on more responsible practices, they could really turn this thing around. They need to stop being part of the problem and become a part of the solution.

We, the unsuspecting American consumers, have been guilty of letting this food travesty go unchecked. We have the power to make real changes, and that power comes from our pockets.

DON'T BUY ANYMORE OF THEIR CRAP and let your dollar speak for itself. Give the food entities a reason to do the right thing.

*　　　*　　　*　　　*　　　*　　　*　　　*

These are the things that you should be buying to feed your families:

FOR YOUR PANTRY:

<u>Unbleached organic flour</u> A staple, and a must. There is absolutely a difference between the real thing and the bleached, bromated, "enriched" starch that is conventional flour. Your baked goods might not be as pretty using organic flour, but your family needs to start eating with their mouths and not their eyes. I buy mine in bulk, from my co-op, but it's also available at Whole Foods.

<u>Organic whole wheat flour</u> Much healthier, but harder to bake with. Many people use only whole wheat flour. I usually combine it with unbleached white flour.

<u>Organic oats</u> Keep them on hand, and throw some into whatever you can. All three stores (Whole Foods, Trader Joe's, Meijer) offer reasonably priced organic oats. They also offer the flavored oatmeal packages, which are a bit more expensive but easy. My daughter likes the maple spice flavor. As mentioned, I try to get my daughter to eat oatmeal every day.

<u>Organic pasta</u> This is not that much more expensive than conventional pasta and is totally worth a few extra cents. Organic pasta is not as rubbery, in general, as conventional, and it will continue to absorb whatever sauce or dressing it's tossed in. It helps

to cool it completely, to stop the cooking process. I prefer Trader Joe's spaghetti and rotini and Whole Food's fettuccine and macaroni.

Organic Rice   I buy brown rice, and I usually have organic white rice on hand as well. The trick to cooking "real" rice is in the rinsing, so rinse thoroughly to avoid stickiness. My nanny sister, who inherited my mother's lusterless kitchen abilities, works now for a family who has complimented her on her rice. Her trick: follow the directions to the letter. We tend to over-heat our food, I think because we're always trying to bend the time warp. If the directions say simmer, then simmer. When I was growing up I had a small children's book that had belonged to my grandmother called "an ounce of patience" (I think). Include that ounce in all that you cook, and rice in particular, and you will be happy with the results.

Organic quinoa   I always have some organic quinoa in my pantry. For those of you not yet acquainted with this grain, it's kind of like orzo, but smaller. It's very palatable (bland) but a good, sustaining little grain. My daughter eats hers with cinnamon, but it can be tossed with salad dressing, or maple syrup, or vegetables, or fruit, or raisins…you get the picture. If you're sick, or having trouble keeping food down, a little quinoa and maple syrup can provide painless sustenance.

I've not really delved into barleys and lentils (although my daughter does love a good lentil soup) and I don't want to be pretentious, so I'll not say much more than once you go organic you'll probably get to know all kinds of fun grains and legumes. I am exploring some now, at home, but the children that I feed at school aren't there yet.

Sweeteners   As organic as possible, and nothing artificial! This includes conventional (fake) maple syrup (have you ever read the label of your favorite "syrup"?) and "corn sugar" (high fructose corn syrup's new moniker).
    Even if you have not yet met diabetes (and chances are, if your parents are still alive, you have) you should become familiar with the

glycemic index, which is actually a means of ranking foods according to their consequent blood glucose levels. Foods that release glucose rapidly have a higher glycemic index, which means that they are providing high levels of sugar into the bloodstream very quickly. This is bad. Foods that release sugar in a slower, more even pattern, are good.

Most fruits and vegetables have a relatively low glycemic index (less than 55). Anything with a glycemic index of more than about 70 is going to be unacceptable for diabetics, and really not good for kids, as these foods will produce manic bursts of energy followed by lethargy, headaches and meanness.

Common sweeteners and their glycemic index are as follows:

Stevia—0
Agave nectar—15-20
Raw honey—30
Cane juice—43
Organic sugar—47
Real maple syrup—54
Evaporated cane juice—55
Raw sugar,/turbinado—65
Refined honey—75
Refined table sugar—80
Succonat--65
High fructose corn syrup—87
Brown sugar--54
Molasses--55

Sugar is actually dark brown. When refining sugar, the "brown" is stripped away, leaving the sweet white powder. The brown stuff is actually molasses, and contains all of the minerals and nutrients. So succonat, which is very brown and a little sticky, has more nutrients, and tastes a bit like molasses.

The nutrient content and the glycemic index are two different things: the glycemic index measures the speed at which that sugar is released into the bloodstream, not nutrition value. Maple syrup and evaporated cane juice have the same glycemic index, but maple syrup is more nutritious, because of its mineral content. I use maple syrup instead of sugar frequently, but it is expensive, so not always feasible. The American Indians apparently took maple syrup on vision quests, as the sweet liquid could sustain them for over a month. I add it to smoothies and beverages, like lemonade, and use it in sauces and cooked fruits.

I always have maple syrup, evaporated cane juice and honey on hand (the maple syrup actually belongs in the fridge). With honey and maple syrup, you should try to buy as local and organic as possible. Most farmers markets will feature at least one syrup and/or honey vendor. Formaldehyde used to be utilized in syrup production but is now prohibited in the U.S., and very few maple trees are actually sprayed with pesticides, but organic maple syrup is usually produced better (the problems with syrup production come in the holes that the sap leaks from, which can become moldy, and from over-production) so buy local and organic if possible. There are two grades of maple syrup, grade A and grade B. Grade B maple syrup is darker, and has a higher mineral count, so buy grade B if you can. Honey is "organic" if the bees are in fields that are not sprayed. Very few honey vendors utilize pesticides, but if you're buying local, you can ask your beekeeper about any pesticides that they use.

Everybody loves sugar. Be smart about what kinds and how much you use. With very small children (under three) it's really good to abstain altogether, if for no other reason than the better food choices that they will make as they grow (my daughter, to this day, really does not like, or crave, sweets, other than fruits, which she eats voraciously.)

Sea salt   Table salt comes from the ground, sea salt comes from the sea. Table salt is more heavily processed than sea salt, usually contains metal compounds to prevent clumping, and is often bleached. Sea salt is sun-dried, which adds a bit of natural iodine. I only use sea salt.

<u>Baking soda and baking powder</u> Be sure these are aluminum free please.

<u>Organic corn starch</u> If it comes from corn I always buy organic.

<u>Arrowroot</u> This is a natural thickening agent that many people prefer to cornstarch. It's good for sauces and fruits, as it is "clear," it thickens at a lower temperature, and it tastes better.

<u>Herbs and spices</u> The key words here are organic and fresh, if possible, and at the very least, not irradiated. The very best thing to do is to grow your own and dehydrate them. The cost is negligible, they're the freshest and most nutritious, they're not irradiated, and it's a great way for kids to eat food that they've grown themselves.

For stronger herbs (oregano, sage, rosemary) hanging herbs to dehydrate them works just fine. Tie them in bundles (not too thick—you don't want moisture, as mold will follow) and hang them upside down for a few days, until they're thoroughly dried, then store the dried herbs in airtight containers. Parsley and basil (if you want dried basil--I prefer frozen pesto) are better laid flat and "baked". If you have a gas oven, you don't even need to turn it on; if you have electric, set it at about 150 degrees. Spread the herbs evenly on a parchment-covered pan, and bake about 40 minutes. Crumble the herbs with your hands and store them in airtight containers.

Most herbs are very easy to grow. They can be grown in large pots if you don't have a garden. Parsley is particularly easy to grow, and flaked parsley is a main ingredient in ranch dip, which may help your kids warm up to homemade ranch (once they do, they'll be hooked.)

At the end of the last school year one of my dearest students gave me a basil plant in a container that sat on my back deck all summer. I LOVE the smell of fresh basil. A few years back, at one of the farmers markets where I sold "Real Cookies" and organic baked goods I was next to the most awesome organic farmer named Katie (Nature's Pace Organics) who used to bring a bucket of basil each week and sit it right next to my tent for me to enjoy. She actually donated what she didn't sell to my lunch program, and I made pesto out of it (another awesome organic farmer, Pat, actually told me how to do this: simply put your basil into a food processor, turn it on, and drizzle a little sunflower oil in as the basil is chopped).

Katie had a boon crop of kale that year, some of which she also donated. I cooked up some big pots of vegetable stock and froze them, thanks to Katie and all of my farmer friends. If you're working on a budget, you might want to hang around at the local farmers markets near the end of the day, as many farmers will sell what they have left at bargain prices, and what you don't eat that night you can throw into a pot and make stock out of.

As for spices, I think that it would be great to have the whole seeds of different spices around and actually grind them up as needed. I watch a lot of food TV, and whenever I see a chef grind his own spices I think, "Oh, how cool, I want to do that." That's as far as that notion goes for me, although I am hopeful that I'll get there someday. For now I use as much organic as feasible. I order many of my herbs and spices from Country Life (one of my food co-ops).

I do buy whole nutmeg, and grind that, because I love the smell, and I really do think it tastes better.

Oils As far as oils go, I use extra virgin olive oil, which should actually be stored in the fridge, and sunflower oil. I have used sunflower oil since I was a child, and now I think it's the most palatable oil that's not from soybean, corn, or canola, all of which are genetically modified and badly over-farmed. If you don't have a nut allergy you can try peanut oil, but I don't love the taste myself. Many people use coconut oil for baking and frying. I haven't used it at school as it's a little too pricey.

And I, of course, use butter, which is refrigerated, but can be left out on the counter or in the pantry for short periods of time. You definitely want to use real butter, preferably organic, although organic butter is expensive. Unfortunately, with the increasing emphasis on rBGH, many dairy farmers are not injecting cows whose milk will stay milk, but still utilizing the steroid for cows whose milk will be butter or cheese.

I am lucky enough to live near a small, family owned store called Peacock's Poultry, where Amish (all natural) butter is available. Price-wise it falls between organic and conventional, and it's the tastiest butter I've ever had.

Trader Joes's and Whole Foods both offer all-natural (no steroids or antibiotics) butter.

Nuts I always keep a variety of organic nuts on hand. Nuts rarely go on sale, but watch for them and stock up if you do find a sale. You should be buying organic, and raw, if possible, and most nuts, especially walnuts, pecans and almonds, should really be kept in the fridge, or even the freezer. Pecans, almonds, peanuts, cashews, and walnuts are staples, as a handful of nuts is one of the quickest, easiest and most nutritious snacks out there. Your child should really be eating some kind of nut each day.

Of course, organic peanut butter takes care of that requirement, and is always on my pantry shelf. My daughter really struggled with the food thing last year, as it was the first time in six years that healthy, nutritious, REAL hot lunches were not available to her (she attended a public high school, her first public school, and I have nothing good to say about that experience, which is yet another, and probably my next book, as I maintain that the public school system in this country is broken). She ended up eating peanut butter and jelly on Trader Joe's multigrain oat bread, a handful of nuts, and a few apples each day. Really, for all-day energy, you can't beat a PBJ, but make sure that it's organic peanut butter and jelly and decent, preferably organic, whole grain bread.

Canned goods I try to always have a few cans of organic pasta and some soups in the pantry for emergencies (days that I just can't cook another meal). These I shop the sales for. It's good to always have some organic vegetable and chicken stock on hand as well. Every store has a vast array of organic and all natural stocks and soups available now. My Whole Foods has an entire aisle of soups, which is easy to get sucked into on a cold winter day. When I began this venture that was different—some items were really hard to find. I make a chicken and stuffing dish (my mother's) that calls for concentrated chicken and celery soups (my mom probably used Campbell's) which were unavailable in organic form eight years ago, and I made my own version. Whole Foods and Trader Joe's now carry organic soup concentrates for baking, and I like to keep a few of them on hand (remember back in the day when a can of cream of mushroom soup was thrown in to just about everything?).

<u>Cereals</u> These are always good to have on hand, and can be found frequently on sale. Granola is one of the quickest real food snacks, and is easy and cheap to make if you don't want to buy it. Organic definitely matters here, and organic cereals are more expensive, but shop the sales, and remember that, though they cost more, they are actually nourishing, not just filling, so you won't need to buy as much.

<u>Organic Snack foods</u> My daughter and I are really not snacky people, so I don't keep much of this around, although we do love our chips and salsa. You will be surprised at how little of this you'll actually need once you switch to real food, as the need to "snack" will dissipate, but if you like to have the stuff around, buy organic, or at the very least, all natural (yes, believe it or not, Lay's classic potato chips fall in that realm--though the potatoes are not organic, they've always been just potatoes, sunflower oil and salt.) Both Whole Foods and Trader Joe's carry their own line of snack foods, not organic but real, and cheaper than their organics. And Meijer actually carries a good selection of organic snacky stuff. We like Staci's chips and Trader Joe's cheesy things and tortilla chips. I use their tortilla chips in the nachos that I serve at school.

If you're trying to make these food changes on a budget, snack stuff is really a good place to start. When your family is eating only real food, the need to snack will abate. Of course, there is a difference between needs and wants, and if your family members are habitual snackers, eating organic can become expensive.

Just like with soda pop, snack food should become a luxury, not a given, and certainly not a staple. A small handful of nuts is just as "filling" and far more nutritious than that bag of chemical-laden flavored tortilla chips, so if sating hunger is the objective, forego the snack food for some nuts and fruit, or a handful of granola. Really, if you're trying to stick to the six-meal plan, and feeding them a healthy, nutritious snack in the afternoon, "munching" until dinner time is nothing more than habit brought on by boredom. Try Origami instead.

FOR THE FRIDGE:

<u>Dairy</u> I think that the pus in the milk is probably enough to make you switch to organic, and I think I've pretty much covered the organic vs. conventional argument. To summarize: your family's dairy should be organic, or at the very least, all natural, coming from cows not injected with rGBH.

While I always have organic milk on hand, I use it more for baking than drinking, and I don't insist that my daughter drink it.

I recently had a student tell me they had last attended a school that required children to drink milk with lunch and I was astounded. The idea that children, especially teens, need, or are required to drink milk each day is a product of one of the most powerful lobbying mechanisms in this country, and not based on health concerns.

I knew of a child once who had terrible stomachaches and wasn't gaining weight and wouldn't eat. It took quite a few visits to the doctor until a health professional asked her how much milk she was drinking. Turns out her mother had been insisting (because she thought she was being a good parent) that her daughter drink three 8-oz glasses of milk each day. The milk was fulfilling her caloric needs but she wasn't growing, because her diet was lacking in essential minerals.

The point is that milk has become a crutch in this country. We somehow feel that if our kids aren't eating any fruits or vegetables, as long as they're drinking milk it's okay. This is a product of dairy farming's commercial marketing apparatus, and it's not okay.

First of all, leafy greens are a considerably better source of calcium than milk, and very few parents actually insist that their children eat any of these. Secondly, many children are diagnosed with dairy "allergies" each year and typically end up healthier than their milk-drinking buddies.

Now, I'm not actually saying don't drink milk, or don't eat dairy (although it's certainly not a necessity, and can contribute to things like sinus issues and acne). I am saying that if your children are eating butter and cheese and some milk in their cereal and some yogurt they are getting enough. If a glass of milk is part of a meal it may fill a child up enough that they don't want to eat their veggies, and given the choice of a glass of milk or a plate of broccoli, nutritionally speaking, I'd go with the broccoli. Add a little butter and shredded cheese to that broccoli and you've had your cake and eaten it too.

Although organic dairy is almost always preferable, in some cases locally produced all natural milk is less expensive, almost as safe, and carries a smaller carbon footprint than, say, organic milk that's been shipped across the country. You definitely want milk that is free of hormones, steroids and antibiotics. Many local dairies feed only grass to their dairy cattle, and, though not certified organic, the milk is just as pure.

Raw milk, and all natural, untreated milk, can often be obtained from local farmers or at the farmers markets.

Yogurt   This is a necessity. Organic yogurt goes on sale frequently, so watch for it. I read somewhere that children should eat five things each day, and yogurt is one of them (the other four being oats or whole grains, green vegetables like broccoli or leafy greens, nuts and fruit.) Be careful when buying yogurt, and read the labels, because many yogurts, especially those marketed as "kids' yogurts" contain artificial colors and a good dose of high fructose corn syrup.

Butter and cheese   As people become more aware of the issues surrounding milk, dairy farmers are selling more natural milk and using even lower quality dairy to produce butter and cheeses. Organic butter and cheese is expensive, so try to find an Amish or local supplier that does not use rBGH. Trader Joe's and Whole Foods both offer their own line of dairy products that are not organic but are at least rGBH-free.

Eggs   Buy organic and free range. You can find eggs at almost every farmers market. These farmers' chickens produce eggs all year, and the farmers often make them available, which is one of many good reasons to get to know your local farmers. The egg has been a much-maligned item in the last few decades, but it's starting to make a comeback, for good reason. The egg is a complete food, and is a great source of protein, much cheaper than good beef or chicken.

Produce   Buy fresh and organic, and buy a lot. It really, really blows my mind how few children eat vegetables. Quite a few are really proud of that fact. Vegetables are an absolutely essential daily requirement. Your children need to absolutely understand this. At some point, if necessary, it needs to become "too bad if you don't like it, eat it." Short of becoming a vegetable drill sergeant, utilize every trick you can to get them in your children (including adding pureed squash to sauces and soups). Every human should eat something green each day. When my daughter and I haven't had our daily dose of green we partake of "green stuff"—the green drinks that look icky but are actually quite tasty. I prefer Trader Joe's Green Stuff, but the Whole Foods green drink is really good too, and there are also some good commercial brands out there. Remember, we're not eating with our eyes anymore.

Veggies should be served steamed, or raw.

In most cases it's actually faster to steam a fruit or vegetable on the stove than it is in the microwave, and there are scores of studies that link microwave exposure to cancers and brain deficiencies. I have a commercial steamer at school and it is absolutely the best thing in my kitchen.

Veggies taste so much better steamed. (This does not mean steamed in a dish in the microwave. I had a student a few years ago who loved, loved, loved my broccoli, which was nothing more than organic broccoli steamed in my commercial steamer, topped with butter, sea salt and a little cheddar cheese. When queried by her mother, I shared my "recipe" with her, and she came to see my steamer. This student had even, on occasion, asked to show her friends the steamer. And that mother said 'I do exactly what you do, but they like yours better', and I said 'You steam the broccoli?' and she said 'Yes, I steam it in the microwave' and I said 'Aha!' It's really not the same.)

Avoid the microwave.

Of course, raw vegetables are preferable whenever possible. Some raw veggies with ranch dip is an easy and really nutritious after school snack. Because most kids are so hungry when they get home from school, this is a good time to get veggies in them, or to try a new recipe, as their hunger will make them more likely to eat whatever you put in front of them.

Fruit is usually an easier sell. Most kids will readily eat their fruit requirement each day. My daughter eats easily three, sometimes five or six, apples each day. Watermelon, oranges, bananas and pineapple are staples, as are strawberries, grapes, plums and peaches when they're in season.

If your child is eating the skin of the produce product, that product needs to be organic. Eat as organic as possible, and thoroughly wash anything that's not.

Condiments and salad dressings   Organic mustard and ketchup are not that much more expensive than conventional, and totally worth the expense. They even taste better. The only bottled salad dressing that I use is Meijer's organic Italian, which I use when baking chicken. I make anything that actually dresses a salad myself. Conventional bottled dressing is really conventional bottled chemicals, and organic bottled dressings can be pricey.

FOR THE FREEZER:

<u>Meat</u>   I don't eat any meat, and my daughter eats very little, and really, that's enough. You absolutely want to eat beef that's organic, or at the very least grass-fed, all natural, with no hormones, steroids, or antibiotics added. Good meat is expensive, but it's better to sacrifice quantity for quality. Conventional beef is really scary, scary stuff (40% of the hamburger in this country is made from sick, rGBH-injected dairy cows that can no longer produce dairy) and I would absolutely forego crappy beef altogether (which means, in essence, giving up fast food).

Chicken is a different story. It is illegal in the U.S. to inject chickens with any kind of growth promoter, and while I vastly prefer Amish chicken (the birds are raised more conscientiously, and it shows—Amish chicken is meatier, and tastes a lot better), crappy chicken is nowhere near as dangerous as crappy beef. That said, organic and free range is definitely preferable, and you certainly don't want to feed your family chicken parts, which means giving up processed chicken foods, like chicken nuggets. Institutions that sell processed chicken things utilize the entire chicken (yes, even the beak). They grind up the whole chicken, and produce this pink stuff that looks like insulation, add a bunch of chemicals and flavorings to make it palatable, and sell it in various "food" forms. Don't eat it.

As I only serve beef and chicken at school, I didn't include any pork or fish recipes in this book. I'm not really a big fan of either, but if you're going to eat pork, I'd make sure it's organic, and given the world's rapidly worsening water supply, I'd only eat farm-raised fish.

<u>Frozen vegetables</u>   I'm not really a fan, but it's true that frozen veggies are often richer in vitamins and minerals, because they're harvested at their peak and frozen quickly. Organic corn is a necessity at school (I use Trader Joe's, and the students LOVE it) and I personally eat quite a bit of frozen organic spinach. I also freeze zucchini—I get it from the farmers at the markets, shred it in the food processor, and spread it in a colander to drain for a good

few hours, then freeze it. I also freeze pumpkin, as it's only available in the fall and I hate canned pumpkin, but that has to be cooked and pureed first. You can also freeze some fruits, like cranberries, blueberries, and even raspberries.

Leftovers My freezer is always full of leftovers. I don't like to waste anything, so I freeze whatever I can. I keep bread heels and leftovers in bags in the freezer, to use in stratas or bread puddings, or for stuffing or croutons, and when I make rice I make extra and freeze it. If you're not sure how an item will freeze up, just try it and see. I make complete use of my freezer.

There are obviously items that I've neglected in this list. This book is really more about HOW to eat than WHAT to eat, and I don't want to dictate your menu to you. What I do want is for you to make a commitment to only feeding your family real food, and hopefully these food guidelines further that cause.

*   *   *   *   *   *

Okay, so you're convinced and ready to join the real food revolution, you have a grasp on what you should and shouldn't be feeding your kids, and when. What next?

You need to engage your entire family. You need to talk with your children. Having this discussion in a non-confrontational manner at a time when they're attentive and happy will make the discussion more productive. You need to talk about the human body, the digestion process, and food. The car analogy is a good one. They need to understand the way that different organs are interrelated, and dependent on each other, so that they can understand why this artificial stuff that they've been eating is so harmful. Talk about brain, tissue and muscle development. Try to be brief and entertaining but informative.

They need to know the "why" of what they are about to embark on. It's considerably easier if they are willing participants, and being upfront with them about food issues will help you on this journey. Remember, this is really the green generation that we are raising. They are already considerably more in-tune with environmental issues than any other generation in our history. They need to be. And they've already heard about high fructose corn syrup. Explain to them why it is such a harmful substance.

By the way, telling a child something is "bad for them" is like blowing stinky air in their direction. The over-used phrase is nothing more than a meaningless fun-sucker. High fructose corn syrup isn't just "bad for you," it's harmful because it limits the ability of the pancreas to function, which in turn inhibits the liver, the organ that aids in sending nutrients to the brain and fiber to the muscles, and high fructose corn syrup tricks your body into thinking it's still hungry so you over-consume this plastic stuff that makes you tired and crabby and lazy and fat and sometimes mean.

One of the first subjects that Waldorf students encounter is farming. There's something very innate about planting a seed, watching it grow and eating it, and when attempting a lifestyle change like this, it's a great place to start. Gardening can be a great way to engage them, and a really good way to get them to start eating vegetables and salads, as greens and tomatoes are among the easiest things to grow. And truly, the healthiest food comes from an organically maintained local or backyard garden.

If gardening is not possible, patronize your local farmers markets. It's good to be able to put a face to the food you're eating. The farmers in this country have traveled a rough road, and they deserve commendation. I have a bumper sticker on my car (given to me by a local farmer) that says "No Farms No Food". We don't need cars or TVs or computers, but we do need food. Locally grown organic REAL food, preferably.

You need to convince, or at least explain to, your children that you are giving up processed foods with those twelve ingredients in them. You are now going to eat only real food. Not that hard, right?

Once you start reading labels you will be horrified by what you and your family have been consuming. All of those words that you can't pronounce and don't recognize are unrecognizable to your organs as well, and their confusion stops them from doing what they're supposed to. Make each member of your family read the label of what they're eating before they eat it. Before you change any of the food you eat, spend a few days just reading to them what it is they are eating. Explain to them that if they can't pronounce, define or recognize an ingredient, they probably should not eat it.

It may not be as easy as just quitting, depending on how much crap your family typically eats. When I made the decision to "go real" I thought, "Oh, I'll just quit". It took me all summer. If you are truly making a commitment to eat real, as organic as possible, food, your body will have some toxins to flush. More so for adults, because they have more years of stuff accumulated in their systems.

I did it the summer after my mother died. Many people make drastic lifestyle changes after losing someone to cancer. 45% of cancers are diet related. My mother's was. Besides eating processed foods, low fat cheese, margarine and enriched bread every day, she smoked and drank a lot of diet cola.

I miss her every day. I don't wish this kind of loss on anyone, and hope that it doesn't take serious illness for people to make these changes.

Her surgeon was a typical medical industry professional, but I did glean one thing from him. He said that what they were finding with cancer now is that it's all about the immune system, that we are all exposed to "cancer" each day, and that the compromised immune systems are the ones that lack the ability to defend against it.

A healthy immune system doesn't just happen. It needs nutrients, and is weakened by chemicals. Eating real food will give you a stronger immune system. Period.

So it was with this in mind, during the summer after my mother passed, that I decided to eschew processed foods and live an organic lifestyle.

Mind you, I had been cooking real food at school for two years, the first one under the wing of Shana, the lovely earth goddess woman who put up with my ignorance. I had found a recipe for chicken fingers that utilized soda crackers, and I remember her pulling the crackers off the shelf and leaving them with a note about hydrogenated oils. I went home and looked up hydrogenated oil on the Internet, because I didn't know what it was or why it mattered. She gently steered me onto an organic path, away from the typical mass-produced fare that I had been indoctrinated into, and I am eternally grateful to her.

During that year I was cooking real meals for lunch and stopping at fast food windows for french fries and diet soda every day on the way home. This was the year that my mother was dying, and it was an awful, awful year.

The next year I lost my mother, Shana moved to Australia, and I took over the lunch program. I was still stopping at McDonald's each night on the way home, and still drinking diet cola like there was no tomorrow.

By the following summer I was miserable, morbidly overweight and depressed, with ankles and knees that hurt so bad I could barely walk, and I knew that I had to make some changes.

I started by ending the caffeine habit, and this took ten days of nail-in-the-skull headaches for me. I then did a Master Cleanse, which I do recommend for adults if they want to start fresh. Then I eliminated high fructose corn syrup, then hydrogenated oils, and by the end of summer I was eating only real food, and beginning to feel better.

It took awhile for me to really feel good. Caffeine and aspartame effect your menstrual cycle, so I had a few hellacious periods. And my joints, my back, my weight, my depression, all began to improve.

The changes in my daughter's behavior and moods were drastic. The crabbiness and meanness stopped completely. She grew. She was always the smallest in her class, and is now among the tallest.

We are both so much healthier and happier than we were six years ago.

It started for me with the conscious effort to avoid those twelve things, and with label reading.

Hopefully I've brought you to this same point—you are now reading labels and are determined to get the crap out of your family's systems. You've gotten the caffeine and aspartame out of your family's regimen and need to rid your diets of the rest of these substances.

Now how do you feed them?

It's family meeting time. It's time to turn off all of the electronic devices (even you, dad). The business of your family's health is serious, and it deserves everyone's attention.

Start by making a list of things that your family members feel that they cannot give up. I know a family who could not give up toaster pastries, so switched to organic ones (much more expensive) and cut back elsewhere. If it's chips and salsa, switch to organic salsa and all natural chips (I like Trader Joe's). Learn to make salsa. Pretty much everything that you eat regularly is available in "organic" form, as mentioned. Things like cereal and pasta are an easy switch—just buy organic. When you've made a list of items that you need that are organic, start shopping the sales. Become a savvy shopper. Many mainstream grocers now offer their own brand of organics, and many offer them frequently at sale prices.

Construct a game plan, and involve everyone in the process. Let everyone pick a meal or two, and produce a monthly menu around it. I know that it seems like a lot of work to construct a monthly menu, but when cooking like this, it's much easier if you have a plan, and making a menu for yourself really helps. If you know what you're going to need for the whole month, shopping the sales becomes easier, as does shopping in general, and this is really helpful when trying to fit an organic lifestyle into your budget.

I highly recommend making as much of your own breadstuffs as possible, and when you are making your own bread you want to use every piece of it. So, for instance, prepare mini cheeseburgers for snack on Monday, soup and roll for dinner, soup for lunch on Tuesday, and the rest of the bread in Wednesday evening's strata or a bread pudding for after-school snack. Try to think in terms of a chunk of time, like a week, and not of individual meals, and make use of everything you've prepared. If you're feeding them healthy food throughout the day, they won't eat much dinner, so send it for next day's lunch.

This is really about cooking, not just recipe reading. When writing this book I had to go back and cook much of this to get correct measures, because I'm one that cooks by instinct. Recipes can slow you down. And remember, real food doesn't have to be elaborate. Real food, kept simple, is the goal, right? And you only need thirty meals, really. Your family needs to warm up to the fact that many meals will get eaten twice, once for dinner, once for lunch in the next day or two. When you throw in some easies, like baked chicken, baked potato and steamed vegetables, it's really not that hard to come up with 20 – 25 (or 10 - 15) meals that you can make that your family likes.

My friend serves an egg strata, coffee cake and bacon once a month for dinner, and it's one of her family's favorite meals. She figures if she makes it more they'll not relish it, and it's one of her easiest suppers.

When I was growing up we had about ten standard meals, not thirty. If you take the little bit of time required to plan a month at a time, at least providing the framework, it really, really makes things easier, and more affordable. Approach it like I approach my job: I know what I'm cooking for the month, I know what to shop for, I'm in a routine, I know how to utilize full amounts of products. Shana resisted this routine, because it got tedious to her, but for me the creativity comes in the actual preparation, and I find it easier to maneuver when I'm prepared.

Embrace cooking. Get a comfortable stool, make TV or music available in the kitchen. Wrap yourself around meal preparation. One of the morning DJs that I listen to was just talking about a stressful day's end that included vegetable chopping, and how therapeutic that was. Warm up to the joy of cooking, and learn to enjoy the process.

This is about learning to cook, about developing habits that will make feeding your family healthy and convenient. Some of those habits include your children, especially your teenagers. Middle school is such an important time. These individuals really need to be nourished, and they're always hungry. They also have boundless energy, and are capable of starting meals and certainly doing the dishes, of which there will be more of, frankly. Being a part of a process is really important at this age. And they need to be pulled away from whatever screen they're staring at. Engage them.

Each year that I've cooked in the schools I've had a problem with middle-schoolers, or, I should say, the administrators have had a problem, because middle-schoolers love to hang out in the kitchen. Nourish this. They love food, and they are comforted by warmth and by the aromas. The smell of homemade butterscotch brownies in the oven can change the day of a teenage girl. And these kids should really warm up to the idea of real food, because, being always hungry, they really do learn to appreciate good food. I've always had a little fan club of eighth grade boys, because eighth grade boys love food. And I'm not saying don't eat brownies, I'm saying don't eat crappy brownies.

So, go forth. Don't eat crappy brownies. Prepare real meals and real treats for your family, and they will grow and thrive and prosper and become the people they were meant to be. Really.

The Recipes

This is the food that I have served at school for the last eight years. It's tried and true. It seems very simple, almost rote to me, but I have scores of people who think I should bottle the marinara sauce and the ranch dressing. People ask me for my recipes all the time, so I decided it was time to comply.

Most of these recipes have evolved over these eight years. They are meant as a guideline, really, as a means to an end. They are intended to get you started down the real food path. They are very simple. I cook simply. Shana loved to try new exotic recipes and different herbs and spices, but me, not so much. I like basic food, and I let the real food speak for itself. And it does. Real food tastes better, and doesn't require all the seasonings and spices that commercial food companies rely on to make their stuff palatable.

Real food smells for itself as well. You won't believe how much better your house is going to smell when you switch to only real food.

Please expand upon and elaborate these recipes to your liking, but don't be compelled to overcook. It doesn't have to be elaborate to be good. A chicken breast baked with some leftover (or organic bottled) Caesar or Italian dressing and a starch or a salad is a great dinner.

I have to confess, I really am not a recipe kind of girl, except when baking, and I'm even learning to wing that now. I'm hoping that this book helps you learn to cook, the way that I learned to cook, so that you don't need a recipe, because, frankly, recipes can slow you down. When compiling these recipes I had to cook off and measure many of the items, because I favor the pinch and dash method. I've left ample room on each page for notations, so as you prepare the foods you can notate what you'd like more or less of.

I also have the incredible good fortune to be cooking in a brand new state-of-the-art kitchen, complete with (commercial) convection ovens. I highly recommend the convection oven. There really is a huge difference, to the point that, accomplished cook that I am, I can't really make a successful meal at home, which must be because of my crappy oven.

I started cooking (Easy Bake Oven notwithstanding) when I was in the sixth grade. Actually, going into the seventh grade. My mother sprained her ankle that summer, near the end of July, canceling our much-awaited east coast vacation, and forcing me into the role of homemaker, much to my chagrin. The last half of my summer vacation was spent in drudgery, as I was forced to clean the house and do the laundry and cook the meals, toiling all day while my brother and sister played in the pool. Poor me.

Really, I was the only one that could have. I took to it immediately, which irritated my already irritable mother, who was not a culinary aficionado. My paternal grandmother was, though, and I started to cook with her whenever I could.

My maternal grandmother was a pretty decent baker, and my mom had a box of her recipes, which became my creative after-school outlet. Her lazy daisy cake was one of my first ventures, and remains an all-time favorite of mine.

The mother of my best friend in eighth grade was a cake decorator, so my creative baking juices continued to flow through junior high. They were Finnish, and her nissua recipe is enclosed. It was my first yeast bread. I haven't spoken to her in years, so I hope she doesn't mind. Thank you, Mrs. Mayry, wherever you are, for allowing us to pore through your stuff, and thus laying the foundation for a lifelong pursuit.

Cooking is a noble pursuit. Feeding your children is your duty, and feeding them well is gratifying on many levels. For me, to be able to do so for these large groups of great kids has been a privilege and a joy. Please embrace the joy in preparing and serving real food for your really great family.

Baby Food

This is a pretty short chapter, but if you're expecting, I strongly encourage this route. Conventional baby foods are just not as healthy. Baby foods (even organic ones) must be heated to such a degree that the food loses up to 60% of its nutritional content.

You don't need to prepare each meal from scratch for them. I used to make up batches of something, like apples or squash, and freeze it in ice cube trays, popping one out at mealtime, which makes the entire process much easier.

Apples are the first food that babies eat, and there's nothing like real applesauce. I can tell you that my daughter's favorite food to this day is the apple, of which she eats many. She also likes the taste of foods, like green beans and broccoli, without butter or ranch dressing, which I also attribute to her beginnings. It's much easier to keep a child on a "real food" path than to adopt one down the road, and feeding your baby real baby food is nowhere near as difficult as you might expect.

In general, and especially with baby food, it's best to avoid the microwave, and, if at all possible, use organic. Really, at this age, they don't need to consume pesticides.

Each of these recipes calls for steaming the veggies or fruits, which entails filling your pan with water up to the floor of the steamer pot, placing food in the steamer thing, topping the pan with a tight-fitting lid, and bringing the water to a boil. When pureeing your baby food, use the water from the pan that you steamed the food item in. It's best to start with the food processor, to make sure that the food is easy for your baby to digest, but as they get a little older, a hand held food macerator works well too.

Real baby food tastes better than processed, and babies really do appreciate a better tasting food. Feeding them fresh vegetables and fruits cultivates lifelong healthy eating habits, and gives you the peace of mind that feeding your children pure, nutrient-dense food affords.

Once your child hits toddler stage you can start adding butter, olive oil, a little fresh grated parmesan, or sweeteners like cinnamon, honey (not until eighteen months) and maple syrup, to their food, although, again, use these sparingly. You do want them to develop a taste for real food, but their palate is becoming more sophisticated, so you can introduce different flavors to them. The flavor should enhance the food, not become the integral ingredient.

Apples (6 months)

Core and slice your apples into six slices. Start with golden delicious apples, as they are the blandest. Steam the apples with their skins on to retain nutrients. Cook the apples about 10-15 minutes, until they are smooshy. Remove them from the heat, remove the skins, and puree them, using the water from the pan to achieve the desired consistency.

Pears (6 months)

Follow the same procedure used when preparing apples. Pears require a bit more cooking time. You can also make pear-apple sauce by mixing the two.

Peaches (7 months)

These you do need to skin first. Immerse them in boiling water for a few seconds and remove them, and the skin will slide right off. Cut them into pieces, removing the pit, and steam them until they're soft. Peaches can be a little tart, so adding a little apple or pear to them might help.

Squish-squash (6 months)

You can bake or steam squash. I prefer baking.

To bake: pierce the squash, throw it in the oven and leave for about an hour. Cool slightly before cutting into it. Scoop out the seeds, cut off the skins, and puree.

To steam: cut open the squash and remove the seeds, cut it into pieces that will fit into your steamer, and steam for about 20 minutes.

A baby's first veggie is usually the acorn squash. It was my daughter's, and she loves it to this day. Squash are so nutritious, and they will stay fresh into the winter if stored properly. I introduced butternut squash next, at about 7 months.

Pureed squash can really become your friend. Adding a little to sauces and soups is a great way to sneak some veggies into your kids, and they'll never know it. Squash are actually very bland.

Sweet potatoes (6 months)

Bake the sweet potatoes at 350° for about an hour, turning them over half way through. Skin, cut and puree them. If you've steamed your squash you can use that water when pureeing. You can also steam sweet potatoes, but potatoes lose a lot of nutrients into the water.

Baked apples

Peel your apples about half way down and core them. Fill the apples with pieces of squash or sweet potato, place the peeled side up in a baking dish and fill the apples with water and, as they get a little older, a drop of maple syrup. Don't overdo this. The sweet tooth really doesn't need any encouragement. Just a drop in the water really does add a bit of flavor, and smells so yummy. As your children grow you can fill the apples with nuts, granola, and raisins, and up the maple syrup. A warm stuffed apple after school on a fall day is welcomed by kids of all ages, I think.

Bake, covered, at 375° about 35 minutes.

Greeny Beanies (7 months)

Snap the bean ends and steam the beans 8-10 minutes, then puree them, using the steamer water. You won't believe how much more palatable the real ones look as opposed to the ones in the jar. They're actually a quite nice shade of green (remember, I grew up in the '70s.)

Pea-wees (7 months)

I didn't love the smell of steamed peas, but they were among my daughter's very favorite foods. Steam the peas for 10-15 minutes and puree them.

Carrots (7 months)

Peel and dice the carrots, steam them about 13 minutes, then puree them. The water from steamed carrots is flavorful and nutritious, so you might want to use it when pureeing some other veggies or sweet potatoes.

Zucchini squash (8 months)

Dice, steam, puree.

Breakfast

A good start to the day is a good thing. Ideally, this first meal should incorporate whole grains, protein (nuts or eggs), fruit, and a good dose of water. Some kind of carb, especially whole grain, is really important for older children and teens. These three necessities (protein, whole grains and fruit) can be combined and served up in many forms, from granola and fruit with milk or yogurt and a cup of fruit juice (100% juice only) to pancakes to a simple egg strata. A decent organic cereal is not a bad way to start the day, especially if you throw in some fruit or juice and some nuts. And remember that a little protein goes a long way. A few nuts or an egg will provide plenty of protein to start the day. The egg is a complete food, and all of the "cholesterol" hoopla about eggs has pretty much been refuted. A scrambled egg on whole-wheat toast (I add a little cheese, and yes, organic ketchup, which I believe came from my father's Hoosier heritage) and a cup of OJ is a great way to start a day.

I have a dear friend that insists on cooking a full hot meal for her brood of five each morning, and I know they appreciate it. I think that this is one of Michele Obama's pet causes—a real breakfast. My daughter, who started high school last fall, informed me then that she felt, as she would not have the benefit of my healthy and hearty lunches for the first time in six years, she would be needing a full cooked breakfast to start the day. I did not oblige every morning, but I certainly didn't want her eating scary school food, and if she felt that she needed a big breakfast to get her through her day, how could I say no?

Pancakes

I serve pancakes with cheese potatoes and fruit salad once a month at school, and it's one of my most popular meals. I sneak some whole-wheat flour into my pancakes (and just about every baked good) at school, and the students are none the wiser. The teachers and parents are though.

These pancakes freeze well, and can be kept in the fridge for a week or two, so it might not hurt to make a few extra and pull them out for an afternoon snack. Throw a few nuts on them for protein and top with fruit or maple syrup (real, of course) and they're a good snack, and of course, a great way to start the day.

1 c. flour
¼ c. whole-wheat flour
2 T. sugar
½ t. salt
2 t. baking powder
1 egg
3 T. sunflower oil
1½ c. milk
½ t. vanilla

Combine the dry ingredients. In a separate bowl beat the eggs slightly, add the oil, milk and vanilla and beat about thirty seconds. Add the egg mixture to the dry ingredients and stir until moistened. Cook in a flat pan or on a griddle.

Variations: blueberry (increase the sugar a little), Hawaiian (pineapple and coconut), banana, strawberry and banana, or cinnamon.

For blueberry pancakes you can add the berries and extra sugar to the batter. Likewise the cinnamon version. With the others, I add the fruit after pouring the batter onto the cooking surface, before flipping.

French Toast

My grandfather's "thing" was French toast. He insisted that the bread be left out all night standing up, so we'd prop pieces of bread up around the kitchen. If you don't want to take this extra step, just use whatever bread you have around. A bread that is more dense will just need to soak in the milk mixture a little longer.

If it's the holiday season you can add a beaten egg to 1 c. of egg nog and soak your bread in this.

3 eggs
¼ c. maple syrup
¾ c. half and half or whole milk
¼ t. salt
1 t. vanilla
8 slices of bread
2 T. butter

In a blender, mix the first five ingredients. Lay the bread in a flat pan and pour the milk mixture over the bread. Let these soak for about five minutes, turn them over, and soak another five. Melt the butter in a skillet over medium heat. Place four slices in the skillet. Resist the temptation to mess with these, keep the heat at medium, and be patient. After about five minutes, flip the toast and smoosh it down just a bit. Continue cooking, flipping one or two more times, until golden brown on both sides.

Potato Pancakes

Okay, I occasionally take a shortcut and use a "processed" item, and this is one of those instances. I use frozen organic hash browns to make potato pancakes. They are expensive, comparatively, but for the extra $3 I'm willing to not deal with peeling, grating, and draining potatoes.

I do like to whip up my own applesauce for these though.

½ c. flour
2 eggs
½ t. salt
½ t. baking powder
1 T. sunflower oil
¼ finely chopped onion (optional)
1 pkg. frozen organic hash browns
1½ T. milk

In a large bowl, beat the egg. Add the oil and milk and stir. Add the dry ingredients and mix thoroughly. Add the hash browns and stir until they are coated. Lightly oil a skillet and heat it to medium. Drop the pancake mixture in spoonfuls onto the skillet. Heat them about three minutes, then flip and smoosh them down. Continue heating and smooshing until they're browned on both sides, about ten minutes.

Applesauce:

5 apples
2½ c. water or apple juice
½ c. maple syrup
1 t. cinnamon

If you want to prep this ahead of time, you can peel and cut the apples and soak them in pineapple juice to prevent browning.

Peel, core and slice the apples. Put the apples and water or apple juice in a saucepan, bring this to a boil, reduce the heat, cover and cook until the apples are soft, about 20 minutes. Add the syrup and cinnamon, cook for another minute or two, remove from the heat and smoosh. You may need to continue adding water while they're cooking to keep them from burning.

You don't have to puree the apples if you don't want to. I have a friend who cooks her apples down like this and fills her crepes with them.

Quiche

I love a good quiche. This is a broccoli and cheddar one, but you can be creative and make any kind you like…bacon and cheese (lorraine, I believe) spinach and mushroom with swiss cheese, spinach and feta, chicken and broccoli, mexican…you get the drift. You could used pot pie pans and make up individual quiches for family members if you like…how fun!

5 eggs
1¼ c. cream, half and half or whole milk
¼ t. salt
¼ t. pepper
½ onion, chopped
2 c. broccoli
1 c. shredded cheddar cheese
1 T. butter
1 T. olive oil
1 piecrust (p.273)

Sauté the onion in the butter and oil. If you're making a version that utilizes peppers or mushrooms, sauté them as well. Place the piecrust in a lightly greased pie pan. Spread the broccoli, sautéed onion and cheese (or whatever fillings you're using) evenly in the pie pan. In a bowl or blender mix the egg, milk or cream, salt and pepper, and pour this into the pie shell. Bake until the quiche is firm when shaken, and cool a few minutes before serving.

Crepes

Crepes were really big for a minute in the late seventies. My dad loved the Magic Pan restaurant (for those of you who missed that fad they had a rotating wheel that had crepe pans on it that they actually made the crepes on. It was really cool.)

For Christmas when I was about thirteen he gave me a crepe pan. If you don't have a crepe pan a frying pan or griddle will work, but crepe pans are optimal.

You can fill crepes with anything, really. They are making a comeback now, I think (in part at least) thanks to the trendy chocolate-nut spreads that are out there now. I like a good chocolate-almond spread in my crepes. These are great after school—just pull out a crepe, spread chocolate nut spread over the crepe, sprinkle with some nuts, and roll this yummy treat up. Of course, served warm with a dollop of ice cream or whipped cream makes this a really simple, really decadent little dessert. Crepes are also good filled with ice cream and nuts and topped with caramel sauce, or even fresh strawberries. A great early summer crepe is one filled with sour cream, brown sugar and fresh strawberries.

3 eggs
1½ c. milk
½ c. water
2 T. melted butter
1 t. maple syrup
1½ c. flour
½ t. vanilla (optional)
butter for the pan

Combine the ingredients in a stand up blender or food processor. Pulse until thoroughly blended and smooth, about 15 seconds. Cover this and let it stand in the fridge for an hour. Melt about 1½ t. of butter in your crepe pan over medium heat. Make sure that the pan is evenly coated with butter then pour about ¼ - ½ c. of batter into the center of the pan. Remove it from the heat and swirl the batter around the pan. You should have enough batter to cover the pan completely. Do this rather quickly (you'll see why). It may take a few tries until you get the right amount of batter. Return the pan to the heat and cook for 60 –65 seconds. Run a rubber spatula around the edge of the pan, loosening the crepe. As soon s the crepe is completely loosened from the pan flip it and cook another 10 seconds. You can keep these in the fridge in a plastic bag or crepe container. You'll need to place parchment paper in between them to keep them from sticking together.

Blintzes

350° 20 minutes

We had a little deli in the neighborhood that I grew up in that made the most unbelievable blintzes. I love mine with cherry topping.

8 crepes
4 oz. softened cream cheese
8 oz. cottage cheese
¼ c. sugar
½ t. vanilla
1 egg (optional)

Beat the cream cheese until smooth. Add the remaining ingredients and mix thoroughly. Spoon an eighth of this mixture into the center of a crepe, fold the bottom and top over the mixture, and roll this up, encasing the mixture in the crepe. Place the blintzes in a baking pan and bake until hot (155°) inside. I like mine topped with cherry pie filling, but any fruit, or just maple syrup or fruit jelly will work as well.

Egg Strata

350° 50 - 60 minutes

I love these. They are a good way to use up extra bread, you can throw pretty much anything in to them, and you can make them up the night before and just pop them in the oven in the morning.

I like mushrooms in my strata, and I top mine with chopped tomatoes, but really, you can add just about anything. If you dice a little zucchini into very small bits and add it it's almost imperceptible, and a good way to get a few veggies into them.

I've also made this with asparagus and gruyere cheese, which may not be exactly kid friendly, but it's yummy. So is a greek strata, with spinach, onion and feta, and topped with chopped fresh tomatoes. Of course, bacon or ham and cheese is probably everyone's favorite, and a good introduction to stratas. If you're making this for dinner or on the weekend, serve with hash browns or o'brien potatoes, and a cinnamon coffee cake, and you're family will sleep happy that night.

3 c. bread, cubed or torn into pieces
6 eggs
2 c. milk
1 t. salt
¼ t. dry mustard (if you don't have this, don't worry about it. It just adds a little zing.)
¼ t. garlic powder (ditto.)
1c. cheese
1 c. broccoli
¼ diced onion (if you have the time to sauté this up before adding it you'll like the taste, but it's fine if you add it raw.)

Spread the bread pieces evenly in a greased 9x9 baking pan. Add the broccoli, cheese and onion, spreading them evenly as well. Mix the eggs, milk, salt and spices in a bowl or blender. Pour the egg mixture over the bread. You can bake this right away or store it, covered, in the fridge overnight and pop it in the oven in the morning. Bake, uncovered, until it's firm.

Granola

250° about an hour

There are a million different variations of this stuff, and it's really easy to make. I'd definitely get the kids engaged in this one, as they will be more inclined to eat it.

I love granola as a topping. One of my favorite meals is bananas and vanilla yogurt and granola. You can also replace the yogurt with syrup.

3 c. oats
2 c. nuts
¾ c. coconut
½ c. brown sugar
½ c. maple syrup
½ c. butter
½ t. salt
1 c. dried fruit (raisins, sundried cherries, cranberries or blueberries)

Heat the maple syrup and butter in a small saucepan over medium heat until the butter is melted. In a large bowl toss the remaining ingredients. Pour the syrup and butter over the granola mix and stir until moist. Spread this evenly on a parchment-lined baking sheet and bake for an hour or so, tossing every 20 minutes to be sure it bakes on all sides.

Breakfast Burritos

Another really easy breakfast, these also make a great afternoon snack.

3 eggs
2 T. milk
½ t. salt
¼ onion
¼ green pepper
2 T. olive oil
1 T. butter
½ t. taco seasoning (optional)
1 diced roma tomato (optional)
¾ c. cheese
2 T. refried beans (optional)
2 soft taco shells (8" homemade or organic)

Chop the green pepper and onion and sauté them in the olive oil and butter. Beat the eggs slightly in a small bowl and add the milk and salt. When the veggies are just tender add the taco seasoning and sweat this for about thirty seconds, then add the egg mixture. Cook until scrambled. Spread a tablespoon of refried beans in the center of a tortilla and sprinkle cheese on top of it. When the eggs are cooked spread them over the beans and cheese and roll this up.

Breakfast Smoothie

Some people add a little flax seed in their smoothies for fiber. Personally, I prefer a handful of granola with my smoothie (on the side, not in it). A smoothie and some granola with nuts is an excellent way to start the day.

1 banana
1 c. pineapple
1 c. strawberries
½ c. orange juice
juice of one lemon
¼ c. maple syrup
½ c. organic yogurt, any flavor

Throw everything into a blender and blend until smooth.

Breads

Pretty much all breadstuffs in the average grocery store are crap, unless they're organic. Some bread companies are now going away from high fructose corn syrup and hydrogenated oils, but are still incorporating the same "enriched" wheat, which is devoid of nutrients, and still utilizing preservatives.

Organic whole grain breads are really the healthiest choice for your children. If you are sandwich people, I'd try to make the switch to organic, which is more expensive, and shop the sales. Bread freezes well.

Or you could make your own. Really, it's not that hard, and it's very cheap. Homemade bread lasts about five days, and up to two weeks in the fridge. Wait, don't close this book. It's not that preposterous a suggestion. I've gotten to where I love to make bread, and actually look forward to my bread-making days. I recently acquired a good stand up mixer (yes, for six years I had done everything with a little hand held mixer or good old-fashioned elbow grease) and they make the process really fast and easy. Homemade bread is also really, really cheap, which might free up some money that you can invest into organic produce or cereal. It's nowhere near as difficult or time consuming as you think. And it's definitely something that you can involve the kids in (or not).

Most yeast breads require five to seven minutes of kneading. I find this therapeutic. I frequently utilize the cool rise method, which means you can basically throw the bread in the fridge and pull it out the next day—no covering for an hour, etc.

I almost always incorporate whole-wheat flour into whatever I'm baking. How much depends on what it is. I also throw in oats whenever I can. I know people who like to throw flaxseed into their bread. If breads like this intrigue you, go with it.

I know people who buy wheat berries and grind their own flour too. I really want to try to grow wheat myself someday, so I can make the process as organic as possible.

I'm also a big fan of muffins, fruit breads and nut breads, which are really quick and easy. Kids of all ages can help prepare them, and most ten year olds can make them pretty much on their own. I did. That's pretty much how I started cooking.

I think these muffins and breads are great for breakfast, with a breakfast smoothie and a handful of nuts, and they're also great as an afternoon snack. If you are able to pop some banana bread or blueberry muffins into the oven so they're still warm when the kids get home from school, I highly suggest you do so. You'll be rewarded on so many fronts if you do.

If you're lucky enough to have no nut allergies in the household, try to incorporate nuts into your baked goods as often as possible. Nuts are really good things.

Basic Breadsticks

400° 6 – 9 minutes

This is a really simple bread stick/pizza dough recipe. I use it quite a bit. Breadsticks are a really quick and easy after school snack, and your teenagers could actually prepare these themselves.

1 t. sugar
1 c. hot (105°) water (your tap water should be hot enough. You
don't want your water too hot. Use a meat
to measure the temp—you should
really have one of these)
1 pkg. (2¼ t.) active dry yeast
1 t. salt
2 T. sunflower or olive oil (I like olive oil for pizza or breadsticks)
½ c. – 1 c. whole-wheat flour
4-5 c. flour
½ t. garlic powder (optional)

In a good bowl add the hot water to the sugar and sprinkle the yeast over the top. Let this stand for few minutes. Don't let it "crust" on top, and don't be afraid to GENTLY stir it just a bit. The yeast should be dissolved and bubbly. Add the salt, oil, 1 c. flour and the garlic powder. Stir this. You want it to be mixed thoroughly and a bit wet still. Give this a good stir, a minute or so, then add another cup of flour. Stir this in. Sprinkle another ½ cup of flour on top and try to start kneading. If the dough sticks to your hands you need a little more flour. As soon as you can smoosh it together without it feeling gooey, take it out of the bowl and place it on a board. Kneading is simply flattening and folding. Use the heel of your hand and push the dough away from you. Fold and repeat. You'll probably need to add flour as you knead.

Here's where the kids come in. Kids love to play with dough. Do this with them, teach them to do it themselves, or you do it, whichever works for your family.

Remember, dough is a very funny thing. It senses your mood. Don't be too rough with it. That said, don't be afraid of it either. It may take a few tries until you get the feel of it, and if your first few attempts are not perfect they're certainly edible, and even enjoyable. Just don't be scared of it.

When you've kneaded the dough for about seven minutes it should be smooth and beginning to feel lighter. Grease a pan or bowl (I usually rinse and dry the original and use that), place the dough in the greased bowl and turn it over, so it is oiled on both sides. You can cover this with a towel and let it rise in a warm oven (if you have a gas oven, just put it in there; if you use electric, then heat your oven to 150, turn the oven off, and then put the bread in) for 30 minutes, or you can utilize the cool-rise method: cover the bowl tightly with plastic wrap and put it in the fridge. Leave it for anywhere from three to twenty four hours.

To prepare the bread sticks pull the dough out (of the fridge or oven, depending on which method you've utilized) punch it down and let it rest, covered, for about twenty minutes if it was in the fridge, about five if it was in a warm place.

On a cutting board, roll out the dough until it's about ½" thick. Using a pizza knife cut the dough into strips (about ¾" by about 3½"). Lay the strips on parchment-lined baking sheets, let them rest for about ten minutes and then put them in the oven. Bake the breadsticks until they are just beginning to turn golden brown on the edges. Try to resist the temptation to open the door while these are baking. When they're done remove the breadsticks from the oven, brush them with melted butter (not margarine) and sprinkle with parmesan cheese.

Cinnamon Bread Sticks

If you have the time to prepare these in the morning they'll replace toaster pastries.

1 c. hot water (110°)
2 t. sugar
1 t. salt
1 pkg. active dry yeast
2 T. sunflower oil
½ c. whole-wheat flour
3 – 3 ½ cups flour
¼ c. finely chopped walnuts
¼ c. sugar
½ t. cinnamon
2 T. softened butter

In a large mixing bowl dissolve the sugar and yeast in the hot water. When it's completely dissolved and a little bubbly add the salt, oil and 1 c. flour. Stir until thoroughly mixed, then let this mixture sit for a minute. Stir it again, then incorporate the whole-wheat flour and another ½ c. flour. Keep adding flour in half-cup increments until the dough pulls away from the side of the pan and doesn't stick to your hands. Turn the dough out onto a flat, lightly floured surface and knead for about six minutes. Place the dough in a lightly greased bowl and turn it over, coating both sides of the dough. Cover this (with a towel) and put it in a warm place for thirty minutes or cover it (tightly with plastic wrap) and put it in the fridge for 3 – 24 hours. After it's risen punch it down and roll it out about ¼" thick (if you're using the refrigerator method you should pull the dough out and let it come to room temperature, about thirty minutes, before you proceed).

Mix the cinnamon, sugar and walnuts in a small bowl. You're going to make eight cinnamon and walnut filled bread sticks. You'll do this by spreading the butter in eight strips across the dough. The butter strips should only go to the middle of the dough (you're going to fold the naked half onto the dressed half). Sprinkle ¾ of the cinnamon/walnut mixture onto the butter strips. Using a pizza knife, cut in between the butter strips to form eight long dough pieces. Fold the naked dough onto the buttered dough and seal the edges. Take each of these eight stuffed breadsticks and twist them a few times, stretching them just a bit as you twist. Place them on a parchment-lined baking sheet and bake. You can either top them with the cinnamon/walnut mixture before you bake them, and drizzle them with icing after they've baked and cooled a little, or you can bake them plain, and when they're out of the oven brush them with melted butter then top them with the remaining nut mixture.

Icing:

½ c. confectioner's sugar
2 – 3 t. milk
¼ t. vanilla

Mix the ingredients together in a bowl. Start with 2 t. milk, and add more if needed to achieve the desired consistency.

Sandwich Bread

400° 35 - 40 minutes

1 c. water
1 c. milk
3 T. butter
2 pkg. (4 ½ t.) active dry yeast
1½ t. salt
2 T. sugar
½ - 1 cup whole-wheat flour
4 – 5 cups flour

    Melt the butter in a saucepan over low-medium heat. Add the milk and the water and heat to 120° – 130° (don't overheat). In a mixing bowl combine the salt, sugar, yeast and 1 c. flour. When the milk mixture is hot enough add it to the flour mixture, and using an electric mixer beat this for about two minutes on medium speed. Add another cup of flour and beat on high for another two minutes. Stir in the whole-wheat flour and the remaining flour, about a cup at a time, until the dough starts to pull away from the bowl. Lay the dough out on a floured surface and knead it for about seven minutes. Cover the dough and let it rest twenty minutes. Uncover the dough and divide it in half. Roll the dough out into a piece that's about ¼" thick and about seven inches long. Starting at the short edge, roll that piece up into a bread "log," tuck in the ends and place it in a greased loaf pan or 13x9x2 pan (you can fit both loaves side by side in a 13x9x2 pan, but they won't have the same shape as the bread that's baked in a loaf pan). Turn the loaf over, so that it's greased thoroughly on all sides. Cover the pan tightly with plastic wrap and refrigerate for 2 – 24 hours. Remove the dough from the fridge about thirty minutes before baking. Bake until golden brown and the bread sounds hollow when tapped.

Dinner Rolls/Mini Cheeseburger Buns

375° 20 – 25 minutes

These are great for mini cheeseburgers, or for breakfast with honey.

½ c. whole-wheat flour
4 – 4½ c. flour
1 T. salt
¼ c. sugar
1 c. milk
1 c. water
1 pkg. active dry yeast
¼ c. butter

Mix three cups of flour, the sugar, salt and yeast together in a mixing bowl. Heat the water, milk and butter to 120° – 130°. Add this to the flour mixture and beat with an electric mixer for three minutes. Gradually stir in the remaining flour. When the dough is not too sticky to knead take it out of the bowl and begin kneading. You may need to add a little more flour as you knead. The dough needs to be kneaded for about 7 minutes. Put the dough in a greased bowl and turn it over (so it's lightly greased on both sides). Let it rise, covered, in a warm place for about 45 minutes. Remove it from the warm place and punch it down. Tear off walnut-sized pieces of dough, shape them into balls, and place them in a lightly greased 13x9x2 pan. Cover and return them to the warm place for 30-45 minutes, then bake.

Nissua

375° 20 - 25 minutes

A slice of this lovely Finnish bread toasted with butter is great for breakfast or afternoon tea.

1 c. milk, scalded
¼ c. melted butter
½ c. sugar
½ t. salt
1 pkg. (2¼ t.) active dry yeast
¼ c. warm water (110°)
2 eggs, lightly beaten
1 t. ground cardamom
4 c. flour

1 egg yolk
2 T. water
2 T. sugar

Dissolve the yeast in the warm water for about 10 minutes, until it's good and bubbly. Add the milk, sugar, salt, cardamom, eggs and 2 c. flour. Beat this until the batter is smooth and elastic, about 3 minutes. Add the melted butter and beat until glossy, another two or three minutes. Stir in the remaining flour. Let this rest, covered, 15 minutes. Knead the dough until smooth and satiny, about 8 minutes. Place the dough in a greased bowl and turn it over, making sure it's greased on all sides. Let it rise in a warm place (125° – 150°) for an hour. Remove the dough from the warm place, punch it down, and divide it into 3 or 6 pieces (you can make one long braided loaf or two short ones). Stretch the pieces into ropes and braid them together. Place the bread braids on a lightly greased baking sheet and let them rise in the warm place, covered, for 30 minutes. Mix the egg yolk and water together in a small bowl. Brush the braid with the egg yolk mixture, sprinkle it with sugar, and bake until golden brown.

Tortillas

You need a little elbow grease for these, as they need to be rolled out pretty thin. They're worth the work.

1½ c. flour
½ c. whole-wheat flour
1 t. salt
2 T. butter
8 – 10 T. warm water

Combine the flour and salt then cut in the butter. Add the water a little at a time, tossing the dough with a fork until a nice dough begins to form. Knead the dough briefly, forming a dough ball. Cover this with a towel and let it rest for 15 minutes. When you're ready to make the tortillas divide the dough into 12 pieces and roll them into balls. Roll each dough ball out on a floured surface. Cook each tortilla individually in a lightly greased skillet over medium-high heat for about 90 seconds, then flip and cook another 90. If you're planning on storing these for later consumption you'll need to place parchment paper between them to prevent them from sticking together.

Muffins

Muffins are a simple and delicious way to fight the real food fight. You'll see that these recipes are all quite similar. It's good to have a basic muffin recipe down pat and create your own variations from there. If you mix the dry ingredients the night before you can have your muffins in the oven in five minutes and in a lunchbox in less than thirty, while enjoying the smell of freshly baked real food while getting ready to face the day. Apple slices and a nice muffin make a terrific mid-morning or after-school snack.

I use standard cupcake pans for all of my muffins. I do use the paper linings, and I prefer the unbleached ones.

Blueberry Muffins

400° 20 - 25 minutes

1½ c. flour
½ c. whole-wheat flour
⅔ c. sugar
½ t. salt
1 T. baking powder
⅓ t. cinnamon
1 egg
⅓ c. sunflower oil
1 c. milk
½ t. vanilla
1½ c. blueberries

Combine and mix the dry ingredients. Add the blueberries. In a separate bowl, beat the egg slightly, add the remaining ingredients, then combine this with the blueberry mixture. Stir enough to moisten (don't whip). Fill the cupcake pans ⅔ full, sprinkle each muffin with a touch of sugar, and bake.

Cinnamon Muffins

400° 20-25 minutes

1½ c. flour
½ c. whole-wheat flour
¾ c. sugar
1 T. baking powder
½ t. sea salt
1½ t. cinnamon
1 egg
⅓ c. sunflower oil
1 c. milk
1 t. vanilla

Combine the dry ingredients. In a separate bowl, beat the egg slightly, then add the remaining ingredients and mix this thoroughly. Add the milk mixture to the dry ingredients and stir just enough to moisten (don't whip). Top with crumb topping and bake.

Crumb Topping:

¼ c. butter
⅓ c. brown sugar
¼ c. oats
¼ c. whole-wheat flour
½ t. cinnamon
¼ c. chopped nuts (optional)

Mix the dry ingredients in a bowl then cut in the butter with a pastry blender.

Cranberry Muffins

400° 20 minutes

These are a holiday favorite.

1¾ c. flour
½ c. whole-wheat flour
¾ t. baking soda
¼ t. salt
¼ c. sugar
¼ c. sunflower oil
1 egg
¾ c. buttermilk
1 c. fresh for frozen cranberries
¾ c. sugar
½ t. orange zest (optional)

    Combine the first five ingredients. Chop the cranberries in a food processor, add ¾ cup (minus about a teaspoon for topping) sugar and the orange zest. In a separate bowl, beat the egg slightly, then add the oil and the buttermilk and mix thoroughly. Add the cranberry mixture to the buttermilk and mix well. Combine the wet and dry ingredients and stir to moisten. Fill cupcake pans ⅔ full, top with the remaining sugar and bake.

Cooking with Pumpkin:

I cook with pumpkin whenever I can. Organic pie pumpkins, even at top dollar, are a real bargain—you get a lot of bang for your buck. They're also easy to grow, provided you can keep them protected from the wildlife. It's easy for very small children to start a pumpkin seed, plant it in the ground, cultivate, bake, prepare and eat it. This is a great way to introduce the seed to stomach to brain process to small children.

To bake a pie pumpkin (it needs to be a pie pumpkin—they are smaller and darker than the jack-o-lanterns) stab the pumpkin with a large knife—carefully—this is one of things that you definitely don't want to engage your kids in. Hold the pumpkin by its stem, and keep the knife's cutting edge away from the stem and your hand. It's really not that scary—pie pumpkins are relatively soft. Stab the pumpkin three or four times, place it on a baking sheet, and bake it at 375° for about an hour. The skin will be hard and fallen away from the pumpkin a bit, and probably starting to brown. You'll be able to smell the cooked pumpkin.

Let the pumpkin cool, then peel the skin off the pumpkin and separate the meat. If you want you can roast the seeds (I highly suggest that you do—I have a very good friend who has been making pumpkin seeds for thirty some years, and has always sworn that pie pumpkin seeds are the only kind worth roasting).

Puree the pumpkin meat in the food processor (you might need to add a little water –you want it to be a little thicker than baby food.)

This freezes quite well, so I prepare a few pumpkins at a time and freeze what I don't immediately use.

To Roast Pumpkin Seeds:

Put the seeds in a colander and rinse them thoroughly, making sure that they are free of pumpkin guts. They need to be dry before you toss them in oil, as any water will repel the oil (duh). Toss the dry seeds lightly with extra virgin olive or sunflower oil and salt. Roast them at 400° for about thirty minutes, tossing a few times as they bake.

Pumpkin Muffins

400° 18-20 minutes

¾ c. flour
¼ c. whole-wheat
2 t. baking powder
1 t. pumpkin pie spice
½ t. cinnamon
½ t. sea salt
¼ t. baking soda
1 c. pumpkin puree
½ c. brown sugar
1 egg
¼ c. milk
¼ c. sunflower oil
1 c. oats

Topping:

¾ c. brown sugar
1½ T. flour
½ t. pumpkin pie spice
3 T. butter

Combine the dry ingredients. In a separate bowl beat the egg slightly, add the remaining ingredients, then add the pumpkin mix to the dry ingredients, stirring to moisten. Fill cupcake pans ⅔ full, top each muffin with topping, and bake.

Apple Muffins

400° 20 minutes

1½ c. flour
½ c. whole-wheat flour
¾ c. sugar
1 T. baking powder
½ t. salt
1 t. cinnamon
1 c. apples
1 egg
¼ c. sunflower oil
1 c. milk
½ t. vanilla
cinnamon sugar to top.

Skin, core and chop the apples. If you soak them in pineapple juice they won't brown. Mix the dry ingredients then add the apples. In a separate bowl beat the egg slightly, add the remaining ingredients, and add this to the apple mixture, stirring to moisten. Fill cupcake pans ⅔ full, top with cinnamon sugar and bake.

Hawaiian Muffins

400° 18-20 minutes

1½ c. flour
½ c. whole-wheat flour
1 T. baking powder
½ t. salt
½ c. sugar
½ c. organic coconut
8 oz. pineapple
⅓ c. sunflower oil
1 egg
½ c. milk
½ t. vanilla
½ t. pure almond extract

Mix the dry ingredients. Add the coconut and pineapple. In a separate bowl beat the egg slightly, add the remaining ingredients, then add this to the pineapple mixture and stir to moisten. Fill cupcake pans ⅔ full and bake.

PBJ Muffins

400° 20 minutes

1½ c. flour
½ c. whole-wheat flour
1 T. baking powder
½ t. sea salt
½ c. organic peanut butter
½ c. sugar
1 egg
2 T. sunflower oil
¼ t. vanilla
1 c. milk
¼ c. jelly
2 T. chopped peanuts
sugar to top

Mix the dry ingredients. In a separate bowl, beat the peanut butter and sugar with an electric mixer. Add the egg and beat another minute, then add the oil, milk and vanilla, and mix thoroughly. Add the dry ingredients to the peanut butter mixture. Fill cupcake cups ⅓ way full, spoon a dollop (about ½ t.) of jelly into the center of the muffins and fill the cups to ⅔ full with the remaining batter. Sprinkle the muffins with sugar and chopped peanuts and bake.

Veggie Muffins

375° about 20 minutes

¾ c. flour
1½ t. baking powder
¼ t. salt
1 T. herbs (I use ranch mix)
3 eggs
¼ c. sunflower oil
1 T. sour cream
1½ c. chopped veggies
⅓ c. cheese

Mix the dry ingredients. In a separate bowl beat the eggs then add the oil, sour cream, veggies and cheese. Add this to the dry ingredients and stir to moisten. Fill muffin cups ⅔ full, top with a little parmesan or cheddar if you like, and bake.

Drop Biscuits

Quick and simple, you can come up with your own family favorites. These are a few of mine. For extra tasty biscuits, sauté half an onion, chopped, in a little olive oil and a little butter and add this to the batter.

Plain Drop Biscuit:

1½ c. flour
½ c. whole-wheat flour
1 T. baking powder
½ t. salt
2 T. sugar
⅓ c. butter
1 c. milk

Mix the dry ingredients. Cut in the butter (even though it's more difficult, the colder the better). Add the milk and stir until blended. Drop the dough by the spoonfuls onto a parchment lined baking sheet and bake.

Olive and Cheddar Biscuits: fold in ¾ c. shredded cheddar cheese and ½ c. chopped green olives.

Bacon and Cheddar Biscuits: fold in ¾ c. shredded cheddar cheese and 6 pieces of bacon, crumbled.

Hawaiian Biscuits: decrease milk to ¾ cup, and 8 oz drained pineapple, ¾ c. shredded Swiss cheese and some chopped ham, if desired.

Veggie Biscuits

450° 10-12 minutes

1¾ c. flour
¼ c. whole-wheat flour
4 t. baking powder
2 t. sugar
½ t. salt
½ t. cream of tartar
½ c. butter
½ c. shredded carrots
2 T. chives
2 T. parsley
½ c. shredded zucchini
1 c. milk

Mix the dry ingredients together and cut in the butter. Add the veggies, then add the milk, and stir until moistened. Drop the dough by spoonfuls onto a parchment lined pan and bake.

Banana Bread

350° 35 – 55 minutes, depending on the pan you use

I serve this at school quite frequently, and I do sell it on occasion at the farmers markets. For Christmas this year I added some mini chocolate chips to a few loaves and gave them as gifts, and a few didn't make it to their intended recipients, as they were so delish I ate them.

1¾ c. flour
¼ c. whole-wheat flour
1 T. baking powder
½ t. salt
⅓ c. butter
¾ c. sugar
½ c. oats
½ c. milk
¾ t. vanilla
1 egg
2 c. mashed bananas (about 5-6 medium)
½ c. walnuts (optional)

Mix the dry ingredients. Cut in the butter, then add the oats. In a separate bowl mash the banana, then add the eggs and beat slightly. Add the milk and the vanilla and mix thoroughly. Combine the wet and dry ingredients and stir until mixed. Pour the batter into a lightly greased or paper-lined loaf pan. You can also bake this in a square pan, which will require about 10-15 minutes less baking time.

Zucchini Bread

325° 45-60 minutes

This is a great way to get zucchini into your kids. All of the squashes are actually quite bland, and so, so nutritious. I actually puree squash and add it to sauces and soups—it thickens them just a bit and is basically flavorless.

I serve this bread as dessert once a month (on taco day) and it has become a favorite among the students. I used to call it cinnamon bread, so they'd not turn their noses up at it, but they're on to me now, and frankly don't care, as they love it. I also sell it at the farmers markets over the summer, and it has developed a nice little following.

2 - 3 c. zucchini, grated
2½ c. flour
½ c. whole-wheat flour
1 t. baking soda
1 t. baking powder
1 t. salt
1 T. cinnamon
dash of fresh nutmeg
2¼ c. sugar
3 eggs
1 c. sunflower oil
1 T. vanilla

Combine the dry ingredients. Beat the eggs and sugar in a separate bowl for about a minute. Add the oil and the vanilla to the egg mixture and stir to incorporate, then add the zucchini. Add the wet ingredients to the dry and mix thoroughly. Spoon the batter into greased or parchment lined loaf pans and bake. You can also make muffins from this batter.

Corn Bread with Honey Butter

400° 30 minutes

1 c. flour
¼ c. whole-wheat flour
½ c. cornmeal
1 T. baking powder
1 egg
¼ c. honey
2 T. melted butter
1 c. milk

Mix the dry ingredients. In a separate bowl beat the egg slightly then add the remaining ingredients. Combine this with the cornmeal mixture and stir just enough to moisten. Spread the batter in a lightly greased 8x8 or 9x9 pan and bake.

Honey Butter:

2 T. honey
2 T. butter, softened

Mix together and spread on a warm baked good. Yum.

Carrot-Pineapple Bread

350° 1 hour

2½ c. flour
½ c. whole-wheat flour
2 t. baking soda
1 t. salt
1 t. cinnamon
½ t. baking powder
¾ t. nutmeg
1 c. walnuts (optional)
2 c. sugar
1 c. sunflower oil
1 T. vanilla
3 eggs
2 c. shredded carrots
8 oz. pineapple, drained

Mix the dry ingredients. In a separate bowl beat the eggs and the sugar for about a minute. Mix in the oil and the vanilla then add the carrots and the pineapple. Add the pineapple mixture to the dry ingredients and mix thoroughly. Pour the batter into a greased or paper-lined 13x9x2 pan and bake.

Pineapple Cheese Bread

375° 55 - 60 minutes, cover loosely with foil and bake another 15 minutes.

2¼ c. flour
½ c. whole-wheat flour
1½ t. dried minced onion, ½ t. onion powder or ¼ fresh onion, chopped and sautéed
1½ t. salt
1½ t. baking soda
1 c. shredded swiss cheese
1 c. milk
⅓ c. sunflower oil
½ c. sugar
2 eggs
1 c. crushed pineapple

Mix the dry ingredients. Add the pineapple and the Swiss cheese. In a separate bowl lightly beat the eggs, add the milk and the oil, mix, and add this to the pineapple mixture, stirring until moist. Pour the batter into a lightly greased or paper-lined loaf pan or 9x9 square pan and bake.

Pumpkin Bread

350° 1 hour

I serve this for dessert on macaroni & cheese/broccoli day. During the fall I cook up as many organic pie pumpkins that I can get my hands on and I puree, portion and freeze what I don't use, as I simply don't love canned pumpkin. Leftovers make great bread pudding, or even French toast, although be careful not to get it too "wet' or it will fall apart.

3 c. flour
½ c. whole-wheat flour
1½ c. sugar
2 t. baking soda
2 t. cinnamon
1 t. salt
1 t. allspice
½ t. baking powder
½ t. cloves
¼ t. nutmeg
1½ c. chopped walnuts (optional)
1 c. sunflower oil
½ c. milk
4 eggs
2½ c. pureed pumpkin

Combine and mix the dry ingredients. In a separate bowl beat the eggs then add the milk, oil and pumpkin. Add the wet ingredients to the dry and mix thoroughly. Pour the batter into a greased or paper-lined 13x9x2 pan (or 2 loaf pans) and bake.

Lemon Basil Bread

350° 50 minutes

My good farmer friend Katy (Nature's Pace Organics) frequently donates leftover basil (among other things) to Real Meals Food Company, and I usually puree and freeze it, but I was looking for a refreshing summer bread to sell at the markets, so I whipped up a batch of this bread, and it sold out. I make it to sell at the markets now during the really hot months, and I always sell out of it.

1¼ c. flour
¼ c. whole-wheat flour
1½ t. baking powder
1½ c. sugar
½ c. butter
one "pesto cube" or 2 T. fresh basil, chopped (I puree in the food
         processor with a drop of sunflower oil)
2 eggs
juice of two lemons
1½ t. lemon zest
⅓ c. milk

Mix the dry ingredients. In a separate bowl cream the butter and the sugar, add the eggs, and beat about a minute. Add the basil and the lemon juice and beat another minute. Mix in the milk. Add the dry mixture to the basil mixture and stir until moistened. Pour the batter into a greased or lined loaf or 9x9 pan and bake.

    This bread can be a bit dry, so I like to wrap it foil after it's baked, and wait 24 hours before serving it.

Cranberry Bread

350° 40 – 45 minutes

2½ c. flour
½ c. whole-wheat flour
¾ t. sea salt
¼ t. nutmeg
½ t. baking soda
1½ c. sugar
½ c. sunflower oil
2 c. fresh or frozen cranberries
½ c. sugar
1 T. orange zest
1 c. chopped walnuts (optional)
¼ c. orange juice
1 c. buttermilk
2 eggs

Combine the dry ingredients. Chop the cranberries in a food processor and add ½ c. sugar. In a separate bowl beat the eggs slightly then add the orange juice, buttermilk and zest. Combine the dry mixture and the cranberries. Add this to the buttermilk mixture and stir until moistened. Pour the batter into 2 lightly greased or paper lined loaf pans or 13x9x2 pan and bake.

Almond Butter Bread

375° 1 hour, cover loosely with foil, bake another 15 minutes.

2½ c. flour
½ c. whole-wheat flour
1 T. baking powder
1 t. salt
¾ t. cinnamon
¾ c. brown sugar
¾ c. organic almond butter
½ c. butter
1½ c. milk
½ t. vanilla
½ t. pure almond extract
1 egg
½ c. chopped almonds (optional)

Combine the dry ingredients. Add the almonds. In a separate bowl beat the butter and the almond butter together. Add the brown sugar and beat this for a minute or two. Add the egg and beat for another minute, then add the milk and the vanilla and mix until smooth. Combine the dry and almond butter mixtures and mix thoroughly. Pour the batter into a lightly greased or paper lined loaf or 9x9 pan. You can sprinkle the top of this bread with some mini chocolate chips if you have some, or some cinnamon-roasted almonds. Yum.

Simple Coffee Cake

375° 25-30 minutes

1 c. flour
¼ c. whole-wheat flour
2 t. baking powder
¾ t. sea salt
¼ t. baking soda
¾ c. sugar
1 t. vanilla
1 egg
1 T. butter
1 c. sour cream

Topping:

¾ c. brown sugar
¾ t. cinnamon
3 T. whole-wheat flour
3 T. melted butter
½ c. chopped pecans (optional)

Mix together the dry ingredients. In a separate bowl beat the butter, sugar, egg and vanilla for two minutes. Mix in the sour cream. Add the dry and wet mixtures together and mix thoroughly. Pour the batter into a lightly greased or paper-lined 8x8 pan, top with the topping and bake. You can double the topping amounts and add a layer of filling in the middle of the coffee cake if you like (pour half the batter into the pan, cover this with a layer of filling, then add the remaining batter and top with the remaining topping).

Salads and Salad Dressings

From what I've seen, about 20% of all kids love salad, another 10% will eat it, and about 70% just won't. This astounds me. What's not to like? I really struggle with this one. I serve pizza and salad twice each month, in an effort to get these kids to eat roughage. I absolutely love a good green salad. I make my own salad dressings, and the more mainstream kids have a hard time warming up to that. They're used to the processed, chemical stuff that they get at home from a bottle, and they somehow believe that the stuff in the bottle is the "right" stuff and are very suspicious of a "substitute." I like fresh dressings, but if you shop the sales you can find some good organic bottled options.

As mentioned, fifth grade seems to be a dietary turning point, and the older children are much better about eating their salads and vegetables, because they're frankly hungrier, and more willing to try different things. The child that has been ordering lunch on pizza day solely for the pizza realizes at about this age that after scarfing down the pizza they're still hungry, and the salad doesn't look so bad. It's really about trying the homemade dressings or Caesar salad, because they almost always love the salads and dressings that I make once they've tried them. The smaller children are just unwilling, usually, to try anything that doesn't look like what their mom serves or anything that is "good for them."

Usually by sixth grade they are all eating their salad. I will continue to struggle with making this happen at an earlier age, and I wish that it came more naturally. I say keep putting a little in front of them and try different dressings and let them tell you what it is they don't like about the salad. Engage them in the process. If you don't say "its good for you" but discuss with them why it is important for that piece of green lettuce to enter their bloodstream, if you and your child are on the same page about food, you will be able to get them to eat a little salad here and there, and a little goes a long way for a small child.

Gardening is a great way to embrace the whole salad/vegetable thing. It's much easier to get a child to eat a salad that they actually had a hand in growing. Tomatoes and greens are relatively easy to grow, and when freshly picked, well, let's just say there is no comparison between store-bought produce that is actually harvested well before maturity, and home grown, picked-when-ripe fresh vegetables. And nothing is healthier, truly, than organic locally grown produce. You can't get much more local than your own backyard.

Greens are so, so, so healthy, and children don't need to eat much to really benefit from them. Salads don't have to be at all elaborate, and a plate of lettuce with some tomatoes, a little cheese, a few chopped nuts and a little dressing is a great meal. Throw in a homemade wheat roll or piece of warm cornbread, and this is a meal that you can't beat.

Ranch Dressing

I used to make this with fresh parsley and chives, but really the dried herbs are easier to use and more acceptable to children, as they seem more like the bottled stuff they're used to. I recommend growing parsley and chives, which you can easily grow in pots if necessary, and dehydrating them.

I also recommend making up large quantities of this stuff (the herbage, not the actual dressing). I have a friend who keeps a bucket of it on hand. You can use it for dip, dressings, burgers, chicken, with butter on a steak, really, just about anything. I actually sell jars of ranch mix at the farmers markets. I gave one to my dear friend Holly, who is the genius behind the Fiddlebumps Apothecary line of organic cleaning and personal care products, and she said that she incorporated it into her meatloaf, potato salad, and even pasta (she tossed it with a little butter and parmesan cheese).

There's a lady who frequents my tent at a farmers market who bought a jar of the ranch mix, made up the dressing, and put it in a commercial bottle, because she wanted her son off the processed, chemical-laden stuff, but knew he would resist. He is none the wiser, but much healthier.

2 T. parsley
1½ t. chopped dried chives
1½ T. garlic powder
¼ t. onion powder—if you can't find organic or all-natural, better
                    skip it.
dash pepper
½ t. sea salt (optional)
½ c. sour cream
2 t. mayo
1 c. buttermilk

Adjust the last three to your preference. For dressing you can use just buttermilk, or omit the sour cream. If you're making dip you can use only sour cream, if you like. I don't use mayo much, but it's necessary to give the dressing the "real" (bottled) taste.

French Dressing

I grew up on French's Catalina dressing, so this dressing brings back a wealth of memories for me. I know it sounds weird, but a salad dressed with french and ranch, in equal parts, is really quite tasty.

1 c. ketchup
½ c. sunflower oil (you can use half sunflower and half olive oil, but it won't last as long)
½ c. cider or white balsamic vinegar
¾ c. honey
¼ t. salt
¼ t. white pepper (I prefer a half-teaspoon for a little zing. You can u use black if you don't have white, and use a little less.)

Mix the ingredients in a bowl or blender (I prefer a blender).

Italian Dressing

¼ c. olive oil
¼ c. sunflower oil
2 – 3 T. white balsamic vinegar
1½ t. sugar
½ t. oregano
¼ t. basil
¼ t. garlic powder
dash of salt
dash of pepper
dash of cumin

Mix the ingredients in a bowl or blender.

Honey Mustard Dressing

1 c. honey
½ c. dijon mustard
1½ T. white balsamic or apple cider vinegar
1½ T. sunflower oil

Mix the ingredients in a bowl or blender.

Maple Vinaigrette

¼ c. olive oil
¼ c. sunflower oil
¼ c. vinegar (white balsamic)
2 T. maple syrup
½ t. dijon mustard

Mix the ingredients in a bowl or blender.

Raspberry Vinaigrette

If you want this dressing to last more than a few days, omit the raspberries.

1 c. fresh or frozen raspberries
⅓ c. raspberry vinegar
¼ c. olive oil
¼ c. sunflower oil
¼ c. maple syrup
1 t. dijon mustard
½ t. tarragon
dash white pepper

Soak the raspberries in the vinegar for a little while, then puree and strain them. Combine the remaining ingredients with the raspberry mixture in a bowl or blender and mix.

Pico de Gallo

2 t. olive oil
1 jalapeno
4 – 6 roma tomatoes
½ onion
1 T. fresh cilantro
½ lime

Chop the jalapeno into small pieces. Remember that the jalapeno's heat is in the innards, so unless you really want a kick to your salsa, just use the outer "meat". In a small bowl, combine the chopped jalapeno and the olive oil. Let this soak for a good minute —up to a few hours. Chop the onion, tomatoes, and cilantro, and add them to the jalapeno and oil. Squeeze the lime over the top and toss.

Salsa

---

1 c. pico de gallo
1 t. tomato sauce

Using a hand macerator or a food processor, grind a bit (as much a you like, really) of the pico de gallo. Add the remaining pico and the tomato sauce and stir.

Michigan Salad

This is my favorite salad to cater—it's so pretty and yummy. Kids can make these up individually for dinner, or make a platter and really impress their friends. You can throw some grilled chicken strips on it and it's a great spring/summer/even fall dinner.

To make it a harvest salad, substitute dried cranberries for the cherries, omit the strawberries, and add some diced celery and carrots. I serve the Michigan salad with raspberry vinaigrette. I dress the harvest version with the maple vinaigrette.

1 head romaine lettuce (hand-torn or chopped with a plastic lettuce knife)
a handful of salad greens
8 strawberries
2 apples, cored and sliced thin (I prefer granny smith, but you can use any apple)
¼ c. sun-dried cherries
2 slice provolone cut in strips (or ½ c. bleu, if that's your bent)
¼ c. walnuts

Put the lettuce and greens in a bowl or on a platter. Sprinkle the sun-dried cherries and walnuts over the top. Arrange the apples slices around the outside of the salad, then arrange the cheese slices around the salad. Put the strawberries in the middle.

Caesar Salad

People who don't even like salad like this Caesar. If your people are salad-haters, start with this. Top it with grilled chicken, steak, salmon or shrimp for a great summer meal.

The Dressing:

¼ c. olive oil
¼ c. sunflower oil
¼ t. garlic powder
juice of ¼ lemon
¾ t. Dijon
¼ c. white balsamic vinegar
¼ c. parmesan cheese

Mix the ingredients in a stand up blender (don't over-mix—pulse just enough to blend thoroughly)

Toss the dressing with:

3 romaine hearts (hand torn or chopped with a plastic salad knife.)
½ c. shredded parmesan cheese
1 – 2 c. croutons

Croutons:

1½ c. cubed bread of any kind
2 T. butter
¾ c. garlic powder
2 T. parmesan

Toss the ingredients. I use my (gloved) hands, and I squeeze the bread a bit so that it really absorbs the butter. Bake the croutons on a parchment-lined baking sheet at 400° until golden (anywhere from 5 to 20 minutes).

Pasta Salad

This is the simplest pasta salad recipe, but the kids really enjoy it.

Remember when preparing this that organic pastas do not get as stiff when cooked, so it's important to cook organic pasta el dente and cool it thoroughly. They also seem to soak up more of the dressing, so I usually dress this salad twice—I mix it up and leave it set for a few hours or overnight (this isn't necessary, you can mix and serve, but I like to let the pasta "harden") then dress it again before serving.

You can always add different veggies according to taste—this salad is good with carrots, broccoli or celery added as well.

1 cucumber, peeled and diced
2 - 3 tomatoes, diced
½# rotini or shell pasta
½ - ¾ c. ranch dressing

Throw everything into a bowl and mix.

Fruit Dip

I absolutely LOVE this dip. I first encountered it at a restaurant that I worked at some twenty-five years ago. It's great with all fruits. I sometimes take the long frilly toothpicks and make little fruit kabobs for the kids, which is an easy and fun way to make a special snack out of fruit, and arrange them around a bowl of this dip.

6 oz. vanilla yogurt
1 c. sour cream
¼ c. sugar
¾ t. vanilla

Combine the ingredients and gently stir until well blended. You can easily adjust this to taste.

Waldorf Salad

I use the fruit dip on the previous page to bind my Waldorf salad. You won't believe how tasty this is.

Of course, if nuts are an issue, you can omit them. When I cater this salad I put them on the side. You can toss them in with the salad, but if not eaten at the initial sitting the walnuts will cause the salad to turn a light shade of mud brown.

4 apples, (I leave the skins on) cored, diced and soaked in pineapple juice
1-2 stalks celery, diced pretty small
one handful of grapes, halved (I try to always use organic)
¼ c. cup sun-dried cherries
¼ c. chopped walnuts
½ c. fruit dip

Combine the ingredients and mix.

Taco Salad

I actually fry my own tortilla strips for this. If you don't feel like that much work, store bought are okay.

To fry tortilla strips, heat 1 cup of coconut or sunflower oil in a saucepan over medium heat. Take a tortilla strip and hold it in the oil. If the oil bubbles when you put the tortilla strip in the oil it's hot enough. DO NOT OVERHEAT THE OIL. I use leftover tortillas for this. Cut the tortillas into strips (3" x ½"). Immerse a handful of tortilla strips in the oil and cook for about 5 minutes. Using a pair of stainless tongs, stir the strips gently a few times to separate them. When they're just turning brown they're done. Remove them with the tongs from the oil. This procedure is simple, but hot oil is always dangerous, so best keep the kids away from this project.

2 romaine hearts, hand torn into bite-sized pieces
¼ c. chopped green peppers
¼ c. chopped onions
3 chopped tomatoes
¾ # ground beef
1 T. water
2 t. taco seasoning
2 c. shredded cheddar cheese
tortilla chips

Sauté the ground beef. You can cook the onions and/or peppers with the ground beef or eat them raw, on the salad. I prefer raw. Drain the beef and add the taco seasoning and water and cook for about five minutes. Arrange your lettuce on a platter. Spread the peppers and onions over the lettuce. I usually put the meat in the center of the salad, pour the dressing around that, and sprinkle the cheese and tomatoes over the top. I then spread tortillas around the edges.

Taco Salad Dressing:

1 c. sour cream
1 c. salsa

My Grandma's Potato Salad

My grandma never, ever gave her recipes out, so I learned to make this with her.

8 potatoes, peeled, cut into smallish pieces, boiled and cooled
6 hard-boiled eggs, peeled and chopped
20 sweet pickles, diced
¼ c. chopped onion
¾ c. mayo
2 t. mustard
1 t. salt
2 T. pickle juice
½ t. vinegar (I prefer white balsamic)
½ t. sugar

Combine the mayo, mustard, pickle juice, sugar and vinegar in a large mixing bowl. Add the potatoes, onion, eggs and pickles. Sprinkle the salt over this, then stir to incorporate.

Oriental Salad

I dress this with honey mustard dressing.

1 head romaine (hand-torn or chopped with a plastic lettuce knife.)
a handful of mixed salad greens
1 can mandarin oranges or 4 tangerines or clementines, sectioned
⅓ c. golden raisin
½ c. bean sprouts
10 – 12 pea pods
1 c. chow mein noodles (if you can't find decent chow noodles,
substitute with chopped cashews)

You can arrange the ingredients artistically, or just sprinkle the toppings over the lettuce and dig in.

Soups

Soups are among the easiest and heartiest real meals that you can put on the table (or send for lunch) and when served with a fresh warm roll, well, enough said, I think. I serve soup and fresh bread on Fridays during the winter months, in part because the parents are invited to eat lunch at school on Fridays and they enjoy this meal as much as their children, and in part because I know that many of them eat (crappy) pizza for dinner on Fridays and I want to get some veggies and protein and whole grains into them so their systems are armed for the onslaught of fast food that weekends often bring. I actually think soup-and-bread night is an awesome replacement for pizza night, and also makes for a great soccer-practice night, last-day-of-vacation night, need-some-comfort-food night, or really, any night.

The recipes included here are my favorites, but really, once you learn to cook real food, you won't need a recipe, and can be very inventive and resourceful in your soup creating. You basically need stock, meat, veggies, and a starch, like pasta, rice, barley or potatoes. With the exception of the stock, any of these may be omitted.

Stocks

Although it is pretty easy to find organic beef, chicken and vegetable stock now, it's even easier to make your own, if you are so inclined. Back in the day women almost always had a pot of stock on the stove. They smell great, and really warm up a cold room on a winter day. When my daughter and I are suffering from congestion, we sometimes start a good veggie stock and breathe the steam. I don't know if the AMA would approve, but it works for us.

If you don't have time to make your own stocks, there are some very nice store-bought options. I love Trader Joe's organic chicken, beef and veggie stocks. You can shop the sales with these (Trader Joe's doesn't have "sales" per se, but Whole Foods, Meijer and Kroger do, and stocks and soups are frequently on sale at these stores). I always keep some on hand.

Though you don't have to use a roux or some kind of thickening agent, I almost always do now. Broth soups and young children, I learned the hard way, don't really do so well together. I once had a student spill hot chicken broth on himself and glower at me, through tears, across the cafeteria. I warmed up to the roux soon after that. A little goes along way, and I love the texture and added flavor.

A stock, a roux, some chicken, some veggies, some beans or lentils, some potatoes or pasta, and you've got soup. Timing is important, and I've learned a few tricks along the way, like boiling the pasta separately, cooling it, and adding it to the soup at the last minute. If you're nervous about soups, follow my chicken noodle soup recipe, and make it a few times, until you start to get to know soups, and take off from there. With these recipes especially, consider them guidelines, and improvise according to your family's tastes. And don't worry about getting it wrong. Over cooked pasta is a little gross, but with anything else in soup overcooking just makes it, well, soupier. Your first attempts may not look great, but they'll taste fine. Serve your soup up with some kind of warm bread, even if it's just a plain drop biscuit. Warm bread as a complement can be very forgiving.

Chicken Stock

water

chicken parts   All-natural, and even organic, wings and drumsticks are relatively inexpensive, and making stocks from bone-in chicken adds calcium to your soup. The owner of the store that sells the Amish chicken that I use swears that the claws from the chicken make the best stock, but you have to be sure you strain thoroughly, because the little toenails must be removed.

You can make chicken stock with just chicken, or you can throw in some veggies, like an onion, celery stalk or leek. Don't chop these up, throw them into the pot whole, with the chicken, a little salt and maybe a dash of pepper, and bring to a boil. After boiling rapidly for 5 – 10 minutes, reduce the heat to simmer, and cover the pot. You'll need to skim off the fat once it starts boiling.

You can leave this simmering on the stove for as long as you like but must adjust the water accordingly. I think two hours is optimal in stock preparation. (A pressure cooker is much quicker, I think.) When the stock is ready you can pour some into small freezer-friendly containers and freeze, if you like.

Veggie stock is the same thing, without the meat. I usually use broccoli stalks, onion and sometimes celery. A few summers ago my neighbor at one of the markets was the most awesome organic farmer, Katie, who that year had a bumper crop of kale, and when she had unsold bunches at the end of the day she donated them to my lunch program, and I made stock and froze it. It was awesome. Kale is a super food, as is broccoli. Onions and carrots can add a little sweetness to a stock. Throw in a little salt and a dash of pepper, boil, then simmer. You won't believe how good this makes your whole house smell.

Cabbage Soup

This is our sure-fire cure for the common cold. Seriously. Water in plenty, sleep, and cabbage soup, and we're almost always good to go the next day.

½ chopped onion
4 c. cabbage
3 c. water
¾ c. veggie stock
1 t. salt
1 t. pepper
1 28 oz. can of diced or crushed tomatoes, or fresh if in season.
1½ c. – 2 c. tomato juice (I use equal parts spicy and plain).

Bring the first five ingredients to a boil in a good soup pot. Reduce the heat and simmer for about an hour. If this soup is being prepared for medicinal purposes, breathe the steam. Seriously. Add the tomatoes, tomato juice, and pepper, reduce the heat to low, and simmer for another 15 – 20 minutes. I truly think that hot cabbage soup on a sore throat is among the most pleasant sensations known to man.

Pumpkin Vegetable Soup

I serve this for lunch each year on the Friday before Halloween, complete with a floating surprise. It's unfortunately not a real favorite, as there's a bit of a tang to this soup that many kids don't like. The kids, and adults, who do eat it, though, LOVE it.

2 T. butter or olive oil
2 onions, chopped
1 rib celery, chopped
1 28 oz. can diced tomatoes
4 c. pureed pumpkin
2 potatoes, cubed
1 c. vegetable broth, or water
1 c. tomato juice
juice of one lemon
2 T. parsley
1 t. salt
½ t. pepper
1 bay leaf
1 c. milk or cream, warmed

Sauté the onions and celery. Add the remaining ingredients, except the cream. As with gazpacho, you can leave this soup "chunky" or puree it. Be sure to remove the bay leaf before you puree. I use one of those hand juicer things and macerate a little, so it's kind of in between. Add the cream after pureeing. This soup can also be eaten cold, but I like it warm with toasted croutons, which for this soup I prepare without the garlic and cheese and I add a little nutmeg or pumpkin pie spice (see toasted croutons, page 135).

Veggie Stew

This is one of the few things that I make that calls for cornstarch. I use it very rarely, and I do use organic, but if you're opposed to cornstarch you can make this with a roux instead. Substitute the oil for butter, add your flour, make your roux, then continue on from there.

Don't let the absence of meat scare you away from this. It's actually a very hearty soup.

¼ c. olive oil
2 stalks celery, chopped
2 cloves garlic, minced
½ onion, chopped
3 potatoes, diced
1 c. chopped tomatoes or 1 can diced
2 carrots, chopped
1 small cauliflower, in florets
1 yellow summer squash, chopped
1 zucchini, chopped
2 c. tomato juice
1 t. organic worcestershire sauce (optional)
1 c. water
1 c. veggie stock
2 T. parsley
1 t. salt
1 t. oregano
½ t. thyme
¼ t. chopped dill
½ t. pepper
2 bay leaves
1 c. frozen corn
1 c. frozen peas
1½ t. cornstarch

Sauté the celery and onion in the oil, add the garlic after about 4 minutes, and continue sautéing for another 4 minutes. Add the herbs and salt and let them sweat a minute or two. Add all but the last three ingredients and bring this to a boil, then simmer the stew for about twenty minutes. Mix the cornstarch with ⅛ c. water and add this to the soup. Bring the soup back to a boil for a minute then add the frozen peas and corn.

Meatball Soup

This is not a light soup. It's a meal in a bowl.

Because I'm a vegetarian, and I'm usually cooking for large quantities, I bake the meatballs on a tray in the oven, make the soup, and add the meatballs to the soup before serving. You can cook the meatballs in your soup pot, remove them, and use the remaining fat to sauté the vegetables if you like. I also cook the pasta separately and cool it, so that it holds up better.

Meatballs:

1# ground beef
½ c. bread crumbs, preferably whole wheat
¼ c. chopped onion
2 T. chopped parsley
2 T. milk
¼ t. salt
⅛ t. pepper
1 egg

Lightly beat the egg. Add the remaining ingredients. I mix this with my hands, and I always wear gloves when handling meat. Form the meat mixture into balls and bake or brown them, depending on which method you prefer.

<u>Soup:</u>

2 T. olive oil (you may need more if you're not using the beef fat)
1 onion, chopped
1 carrot, chopped
2 stalks celery, chopped
1 clove garlic, chopped
1 can diced or crushed tomatoes
1 6 oz. can tomato paste
2 c. water
1 c. tomato juice
1 t. salt
1 t. oregano
¼ t. rosemary
2 bay leaves
¾ c. uncooked or 1½ c. cooked corkscrew pasta
1 c. chopped spinach
parmesan cheese to top

Sauté the onion, celery and carrot in the oil. Add the garlic after about 4 minutes and sauté for another 4 minutes. Add the herbs and salt and sweat this for about a minute. Add all of the remaining ingredients except the pasta and the spinach. If you have not precooked the pasta add it to the soup when you add the meatballs, about 12 minutes before serving. About five minutes before serving add the spinach if it's frozen. If you're using fresh, add it right before serving. Top with freshly grated parmesan.

Chili

This is a very simple recipe, but I find the simpler the better with chili. Elaborate chilies may seem awesome to us, but some of the textures will be deal breakers for many children. Served with cornbread and honey butter, this makes a simple but hearty winter meal. It is my family's traditional Christmas Eve dinner.

1# ground beef
½ onion chopped
1 T. chili powder
½ t. salt
½ t. pepper
dash cayenne pepper
dash red pepper flakes (optional)
½ can diced or crushed tomatoes (optional)
2¼ c. tomato juice
2 c. kidney beans—canned are okay, or if you're working on a
                              budget, do your own.
½ t. brown sugar

Cook the beef and onion in a pot over medium heat. Drain the fat, add the chili powder, salt and peppers and sweat the spices for a minute or two. Add the remaining ingredients and bring this to a boil, then reduce the heat and simmer for about an hour, stirring occasionally.

Vegetarian Chili

½ onion chopped
2 T. olive oil
1 T. chili powder
½ t. salt
½ t. pepper
dash cayenne
dash red pepper flakes (optional)
2 c. (1 can) kidney beans
2 c. chopped zucchini or summer squash
2½ c. tomato juice

Sauté the onion in the olive oil. Add the chili powder, salt and the peppers, and sweat this for a minute or two. Add the kidney beans and tomato juice. Cook over medium heat for 15 – 30 minutes, then add the zucchini and cook another 10 or 15 minutes. I serve this with a dollop of sour cream and a little shredded cheddar cheese.

Tomato-Basil Soup

1 c. tomato juice
1½ c. crushed tomatoes
1 c. veggie or chicken stock
18 fresh basil leaves, minced
1 c. cream, warmed

Heat the tomatoes, stock, and tomato juice in a saucepan over medium-high heat. When this boils add the basil and reduce the heat. Simmer this for about twenty minutes then add the cream.

Roux Soups

A roux is really a food paste. It adds texture to your soup. I always use butter, but I've seen TV chefs use olive oil. You can use a combination of the two. I almost always sauté some kind of vegetable, usually onion at least, in the butter and then add the flour.

I don't know why people got away from the roux. Was it because people thought butter was the devil? It's not. Just think, if you grew your own wheat and made flour and had a cow and made butter— you'd be the master of what you ate!!

You need to butter up to the roux. All those packages of stuff that you buy to make a meal are thickening agents and spices, with a heavy dose of chemicals and irradiation added. Flour, butter, and maybe some onion or celery or pepper combination, or some pure corn or potato starch and water are all you need to cook with. Save yourself some money and some brain cells.

A roux is simply equal parts fat and flour. Melt the butter at very low heat—remember how easily butter burns. Add the flour. It will make a kind of paste. Cook this on low for about five minutes, stirring judiciously. That's it.

Roux plus stock equals soup. If you let a roux sit and cool for a minute then add to it meat stocks you have gravy. It is really easy to come home from work, cook up a simple roux, add some stock, veggies, meat, potatoes or pasta, and have a meal.

Broccoli Soup

2 broccoli stalks
a few pieces of onion
6 c. water
2 c. veggie stock
1 t. salt
½ c. butter
½ c. flour
¼ onion, chopped
4 c. broccoli florets
3 potatoes, peeled and chopped
¼ c. cream, half and half, or milk.

Prepare your stock by cooking the broccoli stalks and onion pieces in a soup pot with the water for about an hour. When you're ready to make the soup remove the onion pieces and broccoli stalks, add the veggie stock, and bring this to a boil. In a sauté pan, sauté the onion in the butter on low heat until tender. Add the flour. Cook this on low for about five minutes then add the roux to your stock. Bring the soup to a boil, add the salt, half of the potatoes and a third of the broccoli. After about ten minutes add another third of the broccoli and the remaining potatoes. In another ten minutes, add the remaining broccoli. When that broccoli is the desired consistency and the potatoes are tender, after about another seven minutes, add the cream, simmer for a minute, and serve. I top each serving with a little bit of shredded cheddar cheese.

Chicken Noodle Soup

12 c. water
4 – 5 chicken legs (I use drumsticks, but parts is parts.)
½ onion, chopped
2 carrots, chopped
½ c. butter
½ c. flour
4 c. organic chicken stock (I like Trader Joe's)
1½ c. vegetable stock (ditto)
about 1 c. chicken pieces, either leftover from chicken strips or
uncooked scraps.
½ # pasta
½ t. pepper
1 T. parsley

Start a good chicken stock. I usually start with a package of drumsticks, a few pieces of an onion, and a carrot or two. When I had all of that great organic kale around I threw a few stalks in. I don't use celery in the chicken noodle soup that I make at school, but you can add it if you like. Bring the chicken legs, whatever veggies you've thrown in and a pinch of salt to boil, then reduce this to a simmer and cook for awhile, at least an hour. (You can have your teenagers start a pot of stock when they get home from school. Seriously.)

If you're using uncooked chicken pieces, add them about twenty minutes before you begin making your roux. Cook the pasta according to the package directions. It should be el dente. Cool the pasta with cold water. I leave it in the strainer in the sink and run cold water on it intermittently to keep it from clumping. In the pan that I cooked the pasta in I make a roux by melting the butter over low heat, adding the onion and cooking until the onion is translucent, about 6-7 minutes, adding the flour, and cooking over low heat, stirring occasionally, for about five. Remove the chicken and vegetables from your stock when you are starting the roux process. I have a hand-held strainer that works great for this. Don't discard the chicken legs. Add the store-bought stock to the pot and bring this to a boil. When the soup boils add the carrots and, if you're using previously cooked chicken pieces, add them now too. Let the carrots cook for about five minutes then add the roux and bring this to a boil.

You need to pick the chicken off the chicken legs. I use my hands, as I need to be certain that I don't let any bones slip through. I always wear gloves, but if you don't have them, make sure, of course, that you use good safe cleaning practices when handling chicken.

Reduce the heat and simmer the soup for about fifteen minutes, then add the remaining chicken, pasta and parsley. Stir and serve.

Potato Soup

This is great with a warm bacon and cheddar biscuit. You can leave out the zucchini if you like, and you can also skip the sour cream. I had a dear friend back in the day whose mother used to make potato-zucchini soup with sour cream, and I just loved it.

5 – 7 potatoes, peeled and chopped, soaking in water
½ leek chopped (I use the tender middle and use the ends for stock)
¼ cup butter, or bacon fat
¼ cup flour
4 c. water
1 c. vegetable stock (you can use half chicken stock if you like)
1 zucchini, cut into small pieces
½ c. sour cream

Boil the leek pieces in water for about thirty minutes. Sauté the diced leek in butter or bacon fat (if you're using bacon, fry it off and remove it from the pan, then add a little butter to the bacon fat, making sure, of course, that the bacon fat/stove top are not too hot for the butter). When the leek is tender, after about seven minutes, add the flour and cook this on low for about 5 minutes. Remove the leek pieces from the stock and add the vegetable broth. Bring this to a boil, then add your roux and stir to incorporate it. Add a third of the potatoes, wait about five minutes, add another third, then in five minutes....you got it. Add the remaining potatoes. Add the zucchini about eight minutes before you're ready to serve the soup. Temper the sour cream before you add it: put the sour cream in a small bowl and add about a cup of soup. Stir to mix, then add the tempered sour cream to the soup.

Corn Chowder

This isn't a quick meal. The chowder needs to simmer on the stove for a good hour and a half.

2 T. butter (or 1 T. butter and 1 T. bacon fat)
½ onion, chopped
3 ears of corn
1 bay leaf
4 c. milk
2 potatoes, peeled and diced
¼ c. chopped red pepper
1 c. frozen or leftover corn

Sauté the onion and pepper in the butter and bacon fat. Add the milk and bay leaf and cook for about fifteen minutes. Break the ears of corn in half and add them to the milk mixture. Cover and simmer for about thirty minutes. Remove the cobs and cut the corn from them. Throw the cobs and the corn back into the pot and simmer this for another thirty minutes. Remove the cobs then add the potatoes and continue cooking until the chowder is thick and sweet. Yum. You can add the frozen or leftover corn about five minutes before serving.

Feel Better Chicken Soup

This is my go-to soup.

1 T. butter
1 T. olive oil
¼ onion, chopped
1 clove garlic, minced (or ½ t. garlic powder)
½ green or red pepper, diced
2 T. flour
4 c. chicken or veggie stock (I use one part chicken and three parts
veggie)
2 c. tomato juice
3 c. cooked chicken pieces
2 c. broccoli
1 t. salt
½ t. pepper
1 c. precooked brown rice

Sauté the onion and pepper in the butter and olive oil. Add the flour to make a roux. Cook the roux over medium-low heat for about four minutes. Add the stock and tomato juice. Bring this to a boil then add the broccoli and chicken pieces. When the broccoli is tender add the rice and cook another 5 – 10 minutes. Season to taste.

Gazpacho

I've always loved gazpacho. My mother made it for me on my birthday a few times. She usually pureed it completely. I sometimes puree about half, leaving some chunks, and I do like a dollop of sour cream with mine. This is a great summer Saturday (after the farmers market) meal.

2 cucumbers, peeled and seeded
1 red pepper, cored and seeded
6 plum or 4 roma tomatoes
1 small onion
3 garlic cloves
3 c. tomato juice
¼ c. white balsamic vinegar
2 T. olive oil
2 t. salt
1 t. white or black pepper
dash of hot sauce, the juice of one lemon, and/or both

Chop the veggies. You can do this by hand or in the food processor, but if you're using the food processor, be careful not to over-process. You want pieces, not mush. In a large bowl combine the vegetables, and add the remaining ingredients. Stir to incorporate, then cover and chill well (overnight is good). Return some (I use about half) of the gazpacho to the food processor and blend to the desired consistency, then toss this with the remaining vegetables.

Entrees

You'll notice how simple these are. You'll also notice that the only meats involved are chicken and beef. I haven't eaten meat in over thirty years (albeit a few really bizarre cravings while pregnant) and can attribute my good health, despite being overweight, to a vegetarian lifestyle. That's not to say that I encourage such in kids, although there are a few who go that way at a young age, and they intrinsically know what to eat, I think. Actually, I think we all do. My daughter periodically (wink, wink) craves red meat, and at that particular time of the month I cook her up a nice grass fed organic steak, topped with butter and sometimes a little ranch seasoning. I don't feel the need to be adventurous when it comes to meat, but if you do, substitute pork or fish. And please don't be fooled by the commercial farming mechanism into thinking that we need meat each day. We most certainly don't. Americans consume considerably more protein than humans should, really. And nuts are actually a better source of protein because they don't accumulate in your system the way that meat does. When cooking chicken or beef it absolutely needs to be all-natural, if not organic. Beef should be grass-fed. Corn is toxic to cows, and as such beef that comes from corn-fed cows is definitely a no-no. I'm lucky enough to live near an Amish community, and as such have access to awesome, local, fresh all natural chicken and beef. Most farmers markets will have local grass-fed beef purveyors, and this is really the best way to go.

One of the realities of cooking real food is dirty dishes. In preparing most of these dishes I typically bake the meat separately, then add whatever sauce, use a pan for a starch and one for sautéing, and that adds up to almost a full load. I suggest running a load while you're eating, so that the kids or husband can unload and reload after dinner. My mother made me unload and load the dishwasher as soon as I could walk, I think, so really, your middle-schoolers are plenty capable.

Chicken Fingers/Nuggets

400° 12 - 15 minutes

These are not the same thing as the processed chicken-like substances found at fast food venues, on your grocers' shelves or in the conventional restaurant. Fast food chicken things have no nutritional value and can be quite harmful. These yummy "real food" alternatives are probably the most well received thing I make, and they're really simple.

Using good, quality chicken is really necessary. I have SO many people ask me how I get my chicken to taste so good, and it really has more to do with the awesome all-natural Amish chicken (from Peacocks Poultry in Troy, MI) that I use than with any prep method.

2½# chicken cut into strips or nuggets
¼ c. sunflower or olive oil (I us a little of both)
¾ t. granulated garlic
¼ c. parmesan cheese
¾ c. bread crumbs
½ c. parmesan cheese

Combine the chicken, sunflower oil, garlic powder and ¼ c. parmesan cheese and mix thoroughly, making sure the chicken is completely covered. You can prepare the chicken fingers immediately or let the chicken sit like this (in the fridge) for up to 24 hours.

Combine the bread crumbs and the remaining parmesan cheese. Dredge the chicken in the breadcrumb mixture. Place the chicken fingers on a lightly greased or paper-lined baking sheet and bake.

Zucchini Strips

400° 14 – 15 minutes

I prepare these in the same manner as the chicken fingers. They are truly one of my favorite things to eat on earth. In the summer I get fresh organic zucchini at the farmers markets, and cook these up. Served with pasta salad, this is a great summer market meal.

3 or 4 zucchini, cut into "fingers"
¼ c. sunflower or olive oil or a combination of the two
¾ t. garlic powder
¼ c. parmesan cheese
¾ c. bread crumbs
½ c. parmesan cheese

Combine the oils, garlic powder and ¼ c. parmesan cheese in a medium-sized bowl. Add the zucchini, tossing to coat. In a flat baking pan combine the breadcrumbs and remaining parmesan cheese. Dredge the zucchini in the breadcrumbs, coating them evenly. Lay the zucchini strips on a lightly greased or paper-lined baking sheet and bake for about 12 minutes.

Chicken Strips

400° 15 minutes

These are the same as the chicken fingers without the breading. I bake these off, put them in a pan with a little chicken stock (for moisture) and cover with foil for a few minutes before serving them. These are on the lunch menu once a month, served with mashed potatoes and steamed carrots, and it's one of my most popular meals. I use this basic chicken for chicken parmesan, chicken palomino, chicken roll-up sandwiches, and I dice and freeze the leftovers and throw them in pot pie as well as my "feel-better" and "chicken noodle" soups.

2½ # chicken, cut in strips
¼ c. sunflower or olive oil
¾ t. granulated garlic
⅔ c. parmesan cheese

Combine the oil, garlic powder and parmesan cheese. Add the chicken, tossing to coat. Make sure that each chicken piece is thoroughly coated. Lay the strips on a lightly greased or paper-lined baking tray and bake.

Zucchini Stroganoff

½ onion, chopped
½# sliced mushrooms
2 T. olive oil
2 T. butter
1¼ c. Italian vegetables (or 2 zucchini and 1 tomato, diced)
¼ c. sour cream
2 T. parmesan cheese
butter noodles

Sauté the onion and mushroom in olive oil for about 5 minutes. Add the Italian vegetables, cover and cook for another five minutes. Stir in the sour cream and cook a minute or two. Serve over butter noodles topped with parmesan cheese.

If you don't have any leftover Italian vegetables on hand, sauté the zucchini with the onion and mushroom and add the tomato when you add the sour cream.

Chicken Pot Pie

Piecrust:

2½ c. flour
½ c. whole-wheat flour
¾ c. butter
¾ t. salt
⅓ c. iced water
4 individual pie pans, lightly greased

Cut the butter into the flour and salt. Add the iced water and blend. Make four larger balls of dough and four smaller ones (larger for the bottom, smaller for the top). Flatten the large balls and roll them out. Place each large crust into a pie pan.

Filling:

4 T. butter
2 T. olive oil
½ onion, chopped
1 clove garlic, minced
2 T. flour
2 c. chicken or veggie stock
1 c. chicken pieces, diced or shredded
1 c. broccoli

Sauté the onion and garlic in the oil and butter. Add the flour and cook this for about five minutes. Add the stock, bring this to a boil, then reduce and simmer. Put ½ c. chicken and ¼ c. broccoli in each pie pan and top each of these with ¼ of the soup mixture. Roll out the remaining dough pieces and top the pies, sealing the dough all around. Flute the edges with a fork. Cut an x into each pie to vent, place them on a baking sheet, and bake.

Broccoli and Cheese Pie:

Follow the same directions as for the chicken pot pie, but instead of chicken and broccoli in the pie use ½ c. broccoli and ¼ c. cheese. You can also throw in a little chopped red or green pepper if you like.

Chicken Parmesan

375° 25 minutes

When I have leftover chicken fingers or strips I sometimes freeze them and pull them out for chicken parmesan. With some freshly steamed green beans and a homemade breadstick—now that's a Real Meal!

2 c. chicken strips, fingers or nuggets
2 c. marinara sauce
1½ c. mozzarella cheese
½# butter noodles

Place the chicken pieces in a lightly-greased 9x9 baking pan and spread the marinara sauce over them. Cover this and bake for about 15 minutes. Remove the pan from the oven, top the chicken with the mozzarella and return it (uncovered) to the oven for another 10 minutes or so. Serve over butter noodles.

Zucchini Parmesan

400° 15-20 minutes

2 zucchini, cut in rounds
2 c. marinara sauce
1½ c. mozzarella cheese
butter noodles

In a lightly oiled baking pan arrange the zucchini flat in one layer. Top with the sauce and bake (covered) about ten minutes. Add the cheese and bake (uncovered) another 8-10 minutes. Serve over butter noodles.

Chicken Teriyaki

4 chicken breasts, cubed
rice, prepared according to package directions
½ onion, julienned
1 carrot, julienned
1 c. broccoli florets
1 c. pea pods

Teriyaki Sauce:

1 c. soy sauce
2 T. brown sugar
2 T. honey
juice of one orange
1½ c. water
1 t. ground ginger
2 t. cornstarch
1 t. finely chopped onion

Combine the cornstarch and the water in a saucepan and mix. Add the remaining sauce ingredients and heat to boiling. Add the chicken, onion and carrots, reduce the heat, cover, and cook about fifteen minutes. Add the broccoli and cook for five more minutes. Stir in the pea pods and serve over rice.

Sweet and Sour Chicken

2½# chicken, cut in pieces
2 T. sunflower oil
1 T. soy sauce
¼ c. pineapple juice
1 onion, julienned
2 carrots, julienned

Sweet and Sour Sauce:

⅔ c. vinegar
½ c. soy sauce
1¼ c. brown sugar
½ c. water
⅓ c. cornstarch
1 t. ginger
1 c. pineapple chunks

Combine the oil, soy sauce and pineapple juice and add the chicken, tossing or stirring to coat. Bake the chicken at 400° abut fourteen minutes. To prepare the sauce combine the cornstarch, brown sugar and ginger in a saucepan. Slowly add the water, stirring constantly. Add the vinegar and soy sauce and cook over medium heat until it boils. Add the vegetables and cook until they are tender. Add the pineapple and simmer this for another minute or two. Remove the chicken from the oven, drain it, add it to the veggies and sauce, stir, and serve over prepared rice.

Chicken and Stuffing

400° 1 hour

I only use boneless skinless breasts at school, but my mother used to get those 'pick of the chick' packs for this meal. My mother did not love to cook, but she had a few good dishes that I still share with the students and this is one of them. She, of course, used canned soup. When I began this hot lunch journey (many moons ago) an organic cream of chicken soup, especially in condensed form, was not to be had, at least in my neck of the woods. There were no boxed stuffing mixes that were not laden with chemicals on the shelves either. Things have changed a lot in the last eight years, thankfully. You can now pick up a package of organic cream of chicken soup and a bag of organic stuffing mix and whip this up in no time.

Don't be afraid of the Swiss cheese. I've served this to many, many a student (and teacher) who hate Swiss cheese but love this dish.

4 chicken breasts, cut in thirds
10 oz. (about 4 cups) stuffing (p. 213)
12 oz. cream of chicken soup concentrate
4 pieces Swiss cheese
½ c. vegetable stock
½ c. milk
½ t. salt

Place chicken pieces in a lightly oiled 9x9 pan. Cut each piece of cheese in half and lay these over the chicken. Spread the stuffing evenly over top. Mix the cream of chicken concentrate, milk, vegetable stock and salt together (I use a stand-up blender) and pour this over the chicken and stuffing. Cover and bake.

Chicken Palomino

This is a favorite among the older students. Palomino sauce is simply a combination of marinara and alfredo sauces.

I like this with pasta primavera, so I steam carrots, zucchini, and sometimes broccoli, or you could use peppers, and toss them with my pasta and a smidge of butter. Top this with the chicken and the sauce.

2½# chicken, cooked
¼ c. butter
1 c. half and half
1 c. parmesan cheese
2 c. marinara sauce, heated
your choice of cooked pasta

To prepare the sauce melt the butter in a saucepan over medium-low heat. Add the half and half and heat to about 200° (just before boiling). Stir in the parmesan cheese, and let this cook for about ten minutes, until the cheese is incorporated, then add the marinara sauce. You can add the chicken to the sauce, or spread the chicken over the pasta and spread the sauce over that.

Mexican Lasagna

375° 35 minutes

I use leftover cheese quesadillas for this. If you don't have any, just layer one tortilla, shredded cheese, and another tortilla.

12 cheese quesadillas quarters, or six 12" tortillas and 3 c. shredded cheddar cheese
1# ground beef
¼ c. onion, chopped
2 T. taco seasoning
½ c. grated cheddar cheese
1½ c. refried beans
¾ c. taco dressing (p. 141)
1 c. homemade or bottled salsa

If you're using tortillas fit them to the pan and trim them so they fit. Save the edges, you can fry them up as a topping for a taco salad. Brown the ground beef and onion in a skillet, drain the fat, and add the taco seasoning. In a greased 13x9x2 pan put four quesadillas on the bottom of the pan, cutting and pasting them until they fit (there should be no holes.) If you're using tortillas, lay a tortilla on the bottom of the pan, cover it with one cup of cheese and top this with another tortilla. Spread the refried beans over the tortilla then top the beans with another quesadilla or tortilla-cheese-tortilla layer. Spread the taco dressing over this tortilla layer, then add the ground beef mixture over that. Top the beef with another tortilla layer. Cover the lasagna and bake about thirty minutes. Remove it from the oven, take off the lid, spread fresh salsa evenly over it, then sprinkle cheese over that, and bake, uncovered, for another 5-10 minutes, until the cheese is melted. Let this sit for five minutes before serving.

Stuffed Peppers

375° 45 minutes

4 green peppers, gutted (slice off top, remove innards)
½# ground beef
2 c. Spanish rice (p. 207)
¼ c. taco dressing (p. 141)
4 tomato slices

If you're preparing the vegetarian version of these omit the beef and add 1½ c. shredded cheddar cheese

Brown and drain the ground beef. You can season this with a little taco seasoning and/or salt if you like. Add the rice and dressing and mix thoroughly. Stuff each pepper with the beef mixture, top each with a tomato slice, place the peppers in 13x9x2 pan and bake.

Marinara Sauce

This is my kid-tested recipe. It's not an extravagant sauce. If you are already using your grandmother from Sicily's recipe, by all means continue. If your spaghetti sauce comes from a jar you might want to give this a whirl. If you've taken my suggestion and grown and hydrated your own herbs, this is a great way to use them. I don't really measure, but I've tried to approximate the amounts. Start from there and adjust the herbage to your family's tastes.

¼ onion, diced
½ c. olive oil
1 t. oregano   (I use ground oregano. I actually ordered this by
                        mistake and figured I should use it up, so I started
                        using it in my marinara sauce, and I like it)
½ t. dried basil or one small basil cube
½ t. garlic powder or 1 large clove
¼ t. salt
1 bay leaf
4# tomato sauce
½ t. brown sugar

Sauté the onion and garlic cloves, if you are using fresh garlic, in the olive oil until the onion is lucid. Remember, burnt olive oil is a carcinogen, so do not sauté this at too high a temperature. "Sweat" the herbs—by this I mean sprinkle the basil, oregano, and garlic powder over the onions, sprinkle a dash of salt on them, and let them cook for about five minutes. Add the tomato sauce and the bay leaf and simmer your sauce for at least thirty minutes, and up to a few hours. When the sauce is hot, add the brown sugar.

Meatza Pizza

375° 15 - 20 minutes

I learned to make this from Miss Doty, my junior high home-ec teacher. Serve with some pasta or breadsticks on the side, and this is a full meal.

1# ground beef
2 t. minced onion
1 t. garlic powder
2 eggs
1 c. bread crumbs.
¾ c. cup marinara or pizza sauce
2 c. Italian cheese (I like the mozzarella/provolone mixes, but you
                    can use just mozzarella if you like)

Prepare the "crust" by lightly beating the egg in a mixing bowl then mixing in the minced onion, garlic powder, beef and breadcrumbs. You can make this into individual "pizzas" or prepare one big one. Flatten the "crust" out completely, top with the marinara sauce and the cheese, and bake until done in the center. A meat thermometer is recommended here—the internal temp should be 155°.

Lasagna

350° about an hour

I use the thin noodles and I don't cook them first.

The Filling:

1 c. small curd cottage cheese
1 c. large curd cottage cheese
1½ c. ricotta
2½ c. mozzarella
¼ c. shredded parmesan
2 eggs
1-2 T. homemade ranch dressing, or 2 t. ranch dip mix and 1½ T.
                  sour cream, buttermilk or milk
3-4 c. marinara sauce
1# ground beef or ½# frozen spinach

    To make the filling beat the eggs in a large mixing bowl. Add the remaining ingredients and stir to mix.

    Spread about a cup of sauce over the bottom of a lightly greased 13x9x2 pan. Place your noodles over the sauce, leaving room for them to grow. Spread half of the ricotta mixture over the noodles. Top this with half of the ground beef or spinach, whichever you're using. Spread a cup of sauce over this, then place another layer of noodles on top of the sauce. Repeat this (ricotta mixture, beef or spinach, sauce, pasta). Cover the top layer of pasta with the remaining sauce, cover and bake.

    I prefer to bake lasagna the day before I'm going to serve it. When it comes out of the oven it's really gooey and tends to fall apart. If you cook it the day before, you can put it in the fridge overnight (don't put it in the fridge hot—it will raise the temp in your fridge and waste energy) and slice it while cold. Before you put it in the oven to reheat it add a little more sauce and some mozzarella if you have it to the top (I add a little shredded cheddar to the topping cheese as well). It takes about thirty minutes to reheat the lasagna. Utilize a meat thermometer to make sure it's hot enough (155°) to serve.

Stuffed Shells

350° 30-40 minutes

1 egg
¾# ricotta
2 c. cottage cheese (I use one c. small curd and one c. large curd)
1 c. mozzarella
¼ c. parmesan cheese
1 T. ranch, if you have some made up, or 1 t. ranch mix and 1 T. sour
                      cream or milk
¼ - ½# spinach

You do, of course, need to cook the shells first. Cook, drain and rinse the shells. To prepare the stuffing, beat the egg in a large mixing bowl, add the remaining ingredients and stir. Stuff the shells with the filling (this will get a little messy—don't worry.) Lay the stuffed shells (open side up) next to each other in a lightly greased 9x9 pan. Cover them with sauce and bake.

Meatloaf

Everyone's mother made her very own version of meatloaf, so I hesitate to include my recipe, as it may not meet with husband approval. Men seem to be very tied to their mom's meat loaf recipe, for some reason.

The students really enjoy this though, so I decided to include it.

2 eggs
1# ground beef
¼ onion, chopped fine, or 1 t. dried minced onion
3 T. ranch mix
½ c. breadcrumbs
¼ c. crushed tomatoes
½ t. salt
¼ t. pepper
2 strips of bacon
1 T. ketchup
1 T. honey
⅛ t. mustard

Lightly beat the egg in a mixing bowl. Add the ranch mix, salt, pepper and breadcrumbs and mix thoroughly. Add the tomatoes and the beef. I mix this all up using my hands, and I always wear plastic gloves.

Prepare the sauce in a small bowl by mixing the ketchup, honey and mustard together.

Lightly grease a 13x9x2 pan. Shape the beef stuff into a loaf. Shallow the middle of the loaf a bit. Pour the sauce in the middle of the loaf and top it with the bacon strips. Bake this until the bacon is cooked and loaf reaches internal temp of at least 155°. It's better to over cook your loaf a little—you don't want it too juicy or it will fall apart.

Swedish Meatballs

The Meatballs:

1 egg
1 T. dried minced onion
1# ground beef
¾ c. bread crumbs
2 T. parsley
¼ t. allspice
dash of nutmeg
½ c. milk
1 t. salt

The Sauce:

⅓ c. butter
¼ c. flour
16 oz. beef stock
1 c. sour cream
1 t. paprika

To prepare the meatballs, beat the egg in a bowl and add the milk, breadcrumbs, onion and spices. Mix this thoroughly then add the ground beef. I mix this with my (gloved) hands, but you can use a good mixing spoon. Shape the beef into balls (you'll probably get about twelve, depending on how big you make them) and place them on a baking sheet. Bake at 375° for about sixteen minutes, until they're done inside.

To prepare the sauce melt the butter in a saucepan over medium heat. Add the flour and paprika and cook this for a few minutes, stirring frequently. Add the beef stock. Bring this to a boil, then reduce the heat and simmer the sauce for about twenty minutes. Temper the sour cream (add some hot sauce to the sour cream and mix) then add the sour cream to the sauce. Add the meatballs and let this simmer for 5 – 10 minutes. Serve over butter noodles.

Spinach and Cheese Pasta

This may sound, (and look) a little weird, but it's easy and super delicious. One of my favorite chefs used to serve the spinach/cheese mixture as an appetizer.

½# frozen spinach
2 c. cottage cheese
¼ c. butter
½ cup shredded or grated parmesan cheese.
½# cooked pasta

Steam the spinach in a little water until it's cooked. Drain it thoroughly. Add the butter and cottage cheese and simmer this for 5 – 8 minutes, stirring occasionally. Stir in the parmesan cheese and serve atop pasta, or even over a baked potato. Yum yum.

Chicken in Parchment Paper

400° 35 minutes

If you don't have parchment paper you can use foil for this, but parchment is more eco-conscious. This is fun for the family, as each person can create their own.

4 chicken breasts, trimmed, and cut into two or three pieces (you can leave them who they just take a bit longer).
4 pieces of parchment paper or foil
4 T. dressing (when I'm in a big hurry I use Meijer's organic Italian with this and throw in some diced green pepper) or 1 T ranch mix.
4 T. water
veggies (optional)

Place a breast in the center of the parchment paper. Top each breast with whatever dressing or spice you're using (you could just put a sprig of thyme or sage on top) and whatever vegetables you like. Add one tablespoon of water. To seal the parchment paper start folding small bits of paper from one side, and make small folds all around the chicken. This needs to be sealed so that no air can escape. If this is too tricky, start with foil, as it is a much more forgiving substance. You need moisture in the package so that the chicken can steam. A little white wine works for this as well.

Chicken Fajitas

This chicken dish can really stand on its own, without all the hoopla. Or, hoopla it up. Homemade tortillas are great with this.

2 chicken breasts, cut into strips
2 t. sunflower oil
1 t. taco seasoning, (or equal parts cumin and chili powder)
½ green pepper, cut in strips
½ onion, cut in strips
2 t. sunflower oil

Mix 2 t. oil and taco seasoning in a bowl (more eco-friendly) or plastic bag (easier-you could try using biodegradable). Add the chicken and stir (or shake) to coat. Sauté the onion and pepper in 2 t. oil. After one minute add the chicken. Reduce the heat to medium-low, cover this, and cook for about 15 minutes, tossing occasionally. Serve on tortillas or pitas with all the trimmings, or just over some rice, or alone, really.

Sweet and Sour Meatballs

This was one of my mom's go-to dishes, and remains a favorite of my entire family's.

1# ground beef
1 T. minced onion
2 T. milk
32 oz. container creamy tomato soup (I use Trader Joe's)
6 oz. (1 can) tomato paste
2 T. minced onion
4 T. brown sugar
4 T. white balsamic vinegar
rice

Combine the ground beef, onion and milk. Form this into balls and bake them at 400° for about twenty minutes. To make the sauce combine the remaining ingredients in a saucepan, stir, bring this to a boil, then reduce the heat and simmer the sauce for thirty minutes. Add the meatballs to the sauce, and serve this over prepared rice.

Cheeseburger Pasta

375° about 40 minutes

The kids at school really love this. If you're adding onion, make sure its incorporated in the beef, not just sitting on top—it needs the fat from the beef to cook.

¾# macaroni noodles
2½ c. cheese
2¼ c. milk
1 T. flour
4 T. butter
1# ground beef
¼ onion (optional)
2 T. ketchup
1 t. mustard
1 c. bread crumbs
1 T. melted butter

Bake the meat (and onion, if desired) in a covered 9x9 baking pan. Boil the pasta in a large saucepan. In a different pan melt the butter and add the flour. Let this cook on low-medium heat for about five minutes, then add the milk and bring this to a boil. Stir in the cheese. When the beef is cooked remove it from the oven and drain off the fat. Add the pasta, ketchup and mustard and stir to incorporate. Pour the cheese sauce over the pasta, cover, and bake this for about thirty minutes. Remove the lid from the pan, spread the bread crumbs evenly over the top, drizzle the butter over them and bake, uncovered, for another 10 – 15 minutes.

Mac and Cheese

This is a quick mac and cheese recipe. I add the sauce to the pasta and serve it immediately. Baked macaroni and cheese, especially organic macaroni, will become very soft, and even start to break down, and this texture is not really what most children are accustomed to.

1# elbow macaroni
4 T. butter
1 T. flour
2¼ c. milk
2½ c. shredded cheese (I like a sharp cheddar and a provolone or jack, but use whatever cheese floats your boat)
½ t. mustard

Boil, rinse and drain your pasta. Melt the butter over medium-low heat. Add the flour and cook this for a few minutes. Add the milk and heat to boiling. Stir in the cheese and the mustard and reduce the heat. You'll have to keep stirring this, or the cheese will clump, and you don't want it to burn on the bottom of the pan. Toss the pasta and the cheese sauce together and serve.

Chicken and Rice

375° 75 – 90 minutes

This is super quick and easy to prepare but takes a long time to bake.

2 large chicken breasts, cut into strips or pieces, about 4 strips or
8 pieces/breast
5 oz. (half of the container) organic condensed cream of chicken
soup (if your family likes mushrooms
you can use cream of mushroom
instead, and throw in a few mushrooms
too)
1¼ c. vegetable stock
1 t. salt
½ t. pepper
1 c. uncooked brown rice
½ c. water
1 T. dried minced onion

Blend the condensed soup, stock and water (I use a stand-up mixer). Spread the rice in a lightly greased 9x9 pan, sprinkle with the minced onion, salt and pepper, and pour in the soup mixture. Cover this TIGHTLY and bake for thirty minutes. Remove it from the oven, spread the chicken evenly in the pan, re-cover and bake this for another 45 minutes or so.

You can add some diced green pepper with the chicken, and throw a little taco seasoning in with the soup mix for a little more pizzazz.

Chicken & Broccoli Alfredo

Trader Joe's makes a pretty decent ready-to-serve alfredo sauce, and it is one of my cheats, although homemade alfredo sauce is really, really good. I find that a penne or fusilli noodle works better for kids than traditional fettuccine, but any pasta will do.

2# diced, cooked chicken
1# broccoli
2 c. alfredo sauce
1# pasta

Boil the pasta. In a separate pan steam the broccoli. Don't overcook it, as it will still be enduring some heat. Throw the chicken into the steamer with the broccoli a minute or two before you're ready to toss it with the sauce. When the chicken is hot and the broccoli is el dente add them to the sauce. Toss this lightly with/or serve over pasta.

Alfredo Sauce:

¼ c. butter
¾ c. cream
1½ c. parmesan cheese
dash of garlic powder

I get the fresh parmesan from my grocer for this. Melt the butter over medium heat and add the garlic and cream. Heat just to a boil then stir in the cheese.

Sloppy Joes

My grandmother used to throw a can of chicken gumbo soup into her sloppy joes, and when I started cooking hot lunch there was not a decent can of chicken gumbo soup to be had, so I made my own. I've amended the process a bit, but I still use a version of that soup. I make up enough of this chicken/rice/gumbo stuff for the whole year and freeze it in one-cup portions.

The Soup Mix:

8 c. water
2 chicken legs
2 chicken breasts, diced
½ t. salt
1 c. uncooked brown rice
12 okra, chopped
½ t. cajun spice
½ t. red pepper flakes

Bring the water, salt and chicken legs to boil and cook for about an hour. Add the chicken breasts and cook for another 20-30 minutes. Remove all of the chicken, add the rice and okra, and cook for 40 minutes. Remove the chicken meat from the chicken legs and chop the chicken into small pieces. Add the spices and chicken to the rice. This mixture should be thick.

Sloppy Joes:

2# ground beef
1 c. chicken/rice/okra soup mixture
⅔ c. ketchup
1 T. mustard
1¾ c. tomato juice

In a large skillet or saucepan cook and drain the ground beef. Add the remaining ingredients, stir and simmer for 30-40 minutes until thick.

Hamburger Stroganoff

This was one of my mother's stand-by dishes. Of course, she used a "seasoning packet" which you could do. I'm pretty sure that Whole Foods sells them.

1# pasta
1# ground beef
½ c. beef broth
4 oz. cream cheese
8 oz. sour cream
½ pkg. condensed mushroom soup
¼ onion, chopped, or 1 T. minced onion
1 clove garlic or ½ t. garlic powder
½# sliced mushrooms (optional)

Cook the pasta. In a saucepan sauté the ground beef, onion and mushrooms. When the beef is cooked and the vegetables are tender drain the fat. Add the cream cheese and mushroom soup and stir to incorporate. Add the beef broth. Heat this until it's bubbly. Temper the sour cream (add a little of the hot beef mixture to the sour cream and mix, then add this to the stroganoff). Serve over pasta.

Mostaccioli

375° about 10 minutes

This is a favorite at school. I serve it with Italian vegetables and breadsticks once a month, and I have a few students, one very dear boy in particular, who counts the days until mostaccioli day each month.

1# penne, rigatoni or mostaccioli, cooked, drained and rinsed
5½ - 6 c. marinara sauce
1 c. mozzarella

Pour the prepared pasta into a 13x9x2 pan. Add the sauce and mix. You'll want it to be a little soupy, as the pasta will absorb some of the sauce as it bakes. Top this with the cheese and bake until it starts to brown.

Side Dishes

French Fries

400° about 40 minutes

Everyone loves these—they take a minute to get used to, because they are not like fast food fries. Here's why: fast food french fries are among the least nutritious foods out there. Food manufacturers typically take potatoes and pulverize them, making a kind of potato-flour mush that they squirt out and cook, then spray with a fragrance that makes them smell like potatoes. They are then fried in hydrogenated oil. They weren't always like that, and they really just need to be potatoes, which is what mine are.

4# potatoes
½ c. olive oil
½ c. sunflower oil
3 T. salt

Peel the potatoes (or don't) and cut them into strips. I cut the potato in half lengthwise, then in half again, then cut it into strips. Toss the potato strips in a bowl with the oil and sea salt, spread them evenly on a lightly greased or paper-lined baking sheet and bake. For crispier fries bake them at 425°.

Oven-Roasted Potatoes

400° 35 minutes

2½# potatoes, cubed
1½ t. salt
½ t. oregano (I use ground)
½ t. paprika
2-3 T. olive or sunflower oil (I use a little of both)

Clean and cube your potatoes. Toss them in a bowl (I wear gloves and use my hands, but a large spoon will work too) with the oil, salt and seasonings. Spread then on a greased or parchment-lined pan and bake. You can toss these with a little parmesan cheese before you serve them if you like.

Twice Baked Potatoes

325° 10 minutes

5 large potatoes
¾ c. milk
3 T. butter
½ t. salt
dash pepper
5 slices cheddar cheese
5 t. shredded cheese

Bake the potatoes at 400° until done. Slice each potato in half lengthwise, scoop out the guts and mash them with milk, butter, salt and pepper. Fill each potato skin ½ full with mashed potatoes, put ½ slice of cheese over the mashed potato, and spoon the remaining potato mixture onto the top of the cheese. Sprinkle with shredded cheese (and scallions or bacon if desired) and bake about ten minutes, until just lightly browned on top.

Potato/Zucchini Bake

375° 40 minutes

2 zucchini, cut in strips or in rounds
1½ c. cottage cheese
2 eggs
1 t. salt
1 c. shredded cheddar cheese
1 c. mashed potatoes

   Par-boil the zucchini (steam them for about four minutes, until just tender). In a mixing bowl mix together the cottage cheese and egg. Spread the mashed potatoes in a greased 9x9 baking dish. Lay the zucchini rounds over the mashed potatoes and sprinkle with salt. Spread the cottage cheese mixture over the zucchini, sprinkle with cheese, cover and bake.

Spinach and Rice

This is another not-that-great looking dish, but it is so good even the pickiest person will eat it if you get them past the appearance. It was a staple in the house of one of the families my sister worked for. She's a very capable nanny, and she doesn't cook much, but what she does cook, she cooks well. That's how she is. I bake up a piece of chicken with Greek dressing in parchment paper to serve with this.

3 c. cooked brown rice
2½ c. fresh or frozen spinach
¼ onion, diced
4 T. olive oil
2 c. crushed tomatoes
1 c. tomato juice
1 t. salt

Prepare the rice according to the directions. Sauté the onion in the olive oil. Add the spinach, crushed tomatoes, rice, salt and tomato juice. Cover this and cook, stirring occasionally, about thirty minutes. Substitute quinoa for the rice for a really nutritious meal.

Spanish Rice

2 T. olive oil
2 T. butter
½ green pepper, diced
½ red pepper, diced
½ onion, diced
2 t. taco seasoning (I use Trader Joe's)
1 t. salt
2 c. tomato juice
4 c. cooked brown rice

Sauté the onion, red and green pepper in the oil and butter in a large saucepan. After about five minutes add the taco seasoning and salt. When the pepper and onion are cooked (not burnt) add the rice and tomato juice, stir to mix, and simmer for about 20 minutes. You may need to add a little more juice or water to prevent sticking.

Refried Beans

---

4 c. beans (they need to be soaked first—follow the directions on the package)
2½ c. water
½ onion, diced
¼ c. butter
2 T. olive oil
¼ t. garlic powder
½ t. cumin
¼ t. coriander or 1 T. chopped fresh cilantro (or both)
½ t. chili powder
½ t. salt

Sauté the onion in the butter and oil. After a few minutes add the seasonings. When the onion is translucent add the water and beans. Simmer until the beans smash easily on the side of the pan (using a spoon, of course) about 40 minutes. Use a potato masher, and start mashing. You may need to add water as you do this.

Fried Mashed Potatoes

This is also a great after school snack.

2 c. mashed potato
1 extra large or 2 medium eggs
¼ c. flour
¼ t. salt
1½ T. ranch mix
1 T. butter or sunflower oil

In a mixing bowl lightly beat the eggs. Incorporate the flour, salt and ranch mix. Stir in the mashed potatoes. Heat the oil or butter in a skillet at medium heat, drop the mashed potato mixture in large spoonfuls onto the skillet and flatten them. Turn the heat up a bit, and flip when browned, after about five minutes. When browned on both sides remove them from the skillet. I top mine with a little shredded parmesan cheese, or (I know this sounds weird) ketchup.

Fried Spaghetti

You can top these with whatever ingredients you like (i.e. pizza sauce and mozzarella, diced tomatoes or mushrooms, salsa, diced chicken and a little ranch dressing, or nothing, really). You can also cut these into wedges and dip them in sauce or dressing.

¼# leftover spaghetti
1 egg
1 c. shredded parmesan cheese
1 T. ranch mix
1 T. sunflower oil

Heat the oil in a skillet (I use my crepe pan for this) over medium heat. In a mixing bowl beat the egg, add the ranch mix, and stir (if you don't have any ranch mix handy add ½ t. garlic powder, ½ t. minced onion, and 1 t. chopped parsley, if you have it). Add the spaghetti and the cheese and toss this until the spaghetti is evenly coated. Spread half the spaghetti mixture in the skillet and smoosh it down a bit. After about seven minutes flip it. You want it to be well browned. If you're making a pizza, when both sides are well browned top with 2 T. pizza or marinara sauce and ½ c. shredded mozzarella, reduce the heat, cover the spaghetti with a lid and heat another five minutes or so.

Italian Veggies

I serve these with mostaccioli and breadsticks, and I use what's left in veggie stroganoff.

½ onion, chopped
5 zucchini, cut into smallish pieces
1 c. chopped tomatoes
¼ c. olive oil
½ c. parmesan cheese

Sauté the onion in the oil. Add the zucchini, reduce the heat and cover, cooking until the zucchini is tender, about 7 minutes. Add the tomatoes, stir, and top with parmesan cheese.

Green Beans and Potatoes

These are great with a steak, or a baked chicken breast.

¾ onion, diced coarsely (not real small pieces)
2 garlic cloves or 2 t. garlic powder.
2 T. olive oil
2 T. butter
2 c. crushed tomatoes
8 golden potatoes, cut in halves
1# green beans
½ c. tomato juice
½ c. water

In a good-sized pot cook the onion in the olive oil and butter. Add the garlic after a few minutes and cook this for another minute or two. Add the crushed tomatoes and simmer for a minute, then add the potatoes. Cook this slowly, covered, stirring occasionally, for about ten minutes. Add the green beans, stir and cover. Simmer this for another twenty minutes, until the potatoes and beans are tender and the sauce is thick.

Stuffing

400° about 20 minutes

3 c. cubed bread
3 celery stalks, chopped
1 onion, diced
¼ c. butter
2 T. chopped sage
¼ t. white pepper
½ c. chopped walnuts or almonds (optional)

Sauté the celery and onion in the butter. In a large bowl mix the sautéed veggies with the bread, chopped sage and white pepper. Spread the stuffing on greased or parchment paper lined baking sheet and bake until golden brown.

Thanksgiving Day Stuffing

350° 30 minutes

4 c. stuffing
¼ c. melted butter
2 c. veggie stock
½ pkg. condensed cream of mushroom, chicken or celery soup.

Pour the stuffing into a greased 13x9x2 pan. In a stand-up mixer or bowl combine the remaining ingredients. Pour this over stuffing, cover and bake.

After School Snacks

These can be served as lunch or dinner as well. They are some of the kid friendly recipes that I serve for hot lunch on a regular basis. They're quick and wholesome, and they're a good way to get the kids on the real food bandwagon, as they are simple and simply delicious. You don't really need to tell them they're eating healthy alternatives, these stand on their own (even the conventional kids love these.)

Most kids come home from school starving, and many gorge themselves on junk food as a result. Good eating habits are really critical at this juncture, so help them out, and have healthy alternatives waiting for them. Because they're usually so hungry it's easier to get them to try different things, or eat some raw veggies and dip, at this point in the day.

Quesadillas

These are so easy and so delicious. I serve them with fresh salsa and sour cream, and corn on the side. You can add some different veggies too, if you like, but I'd sauté any onions or peppers that you might add, as they only cook on the grill (or in the pan) for a minute, and the veggies, if added raw, will still be quite crisp.

These are better prepared on a flat griddle if you have one, but a frying pan is fine too. Depending on what kind of pan it is, it may need a very light coating of sunflower oil to keep the tortillas from sticking.

A good tortilla is very hard to find. If you feel like making them, they're so soft and delicious, and actually quite simple (p. 99). This is a good fun project to engage the whole family in. If you're buying them, read the labels. Pretty much every conventional tortilla is loaded with chemicals, preservatives, and hydrogenated oils. Trader Joe's and Whole Foods both offer good alternatives.

For each quesadilla you will need:

two 8" tortillas
1 c. cheese (I use a combination of cheddar with a little provolone
            and mozzarella, but you can use just cheddar, or any
            combination of cheeses, really)
1 c. chicken, cooked and diced (I use pieces that I've saved and
                        frozen)
OR
½ c. fresh pico de gallo

Heat your skillet on medium for a minute, then place a tortilla in the pan. Spread the cheese and chicken or pico evenly over the tortilla and top this with another tortilla. Before you flip it press the top tortilla down, so that the melted cheese can hold the quesadilla together. Flip after about a minute, and cook until it starts to brown.

Cut the quesadilla into wedges, and serve with sour cream and salsa.

Pizzadillas

These are a big hit at school. Kids love anything that resembles pizza, and these are really quick and easy.

For one pizzadilla you will need:

two 8" or 10" Tortillas
1 - 2 T. pizza Sauce (I use marinara, and add a bit of tomato paste to thicken it a little, but just plain marinara is fine too)
½ c. mozzarella cheese
2 T. cheddar cheese
parmesan cheese

Depending on what kind of skillet you're using you many need to lightly grease it. Place a tortilla in the skillet. Spread the sauce evenly over the tortilla. Sprinkle the mozzarella and cheddar cheeses evenly over the tortilla and top this with another tortilla. After about a minute press the top tortilla down into the pizzadilla so that the melted cheese will hold it together, then flip and cook it for another minute or two, until it begins to brown. Remove the pizzadilla from the pan, cut it into wedges and sprinkle it with parmesan cheese.

Pita Pizzas

375° about five minutes

You could use English muffins or bagels for these. They are simple and quite popular. Whole Foods sells a sandwich-size (4") pita that is perfect for these, and very reasonably priced.

6 pitas
½ c. marinara or pizza sauce
½ c. mozzarella cheese
1 T. cheddar cheese

Top each pita with 1 T. sauce, 1 T. mozzarella cheese and a little cheddar, and bake until the cheese is melty. Don't overcook these, as the pitas will get crisp rather quickly.

Nachos

These are so easy to cook up and are such a welcome treat after school. They're also a great way to get some veggies into them.

Both Whole Foods and Trader Joe's carry good organic or all natural taco seasoning mixes. You can always use a little chili powder, a dash of cumin and a smattering of ground red pepper if you don't have a good taco seasoning option.

1½ # ground beef
1 c. (½ can) refried beans   I use canned at school, as organic refried beans are readily available and reasonably priced, but homemade are not at all difficult to prepare and really delicious (p. 208)
½ c. water
¼ pkg. taco seasoning
12 oz. tortilla chips
4 c. cheddar cheese

Toppings:
shredded lettuce
chopped onions
diced tomatoes
chopped green pepper
jalapenos
homemade salsa
sour cream

Brown the beef in a saucepan. Drain the fat. Add the beans, water and taco seasoning and stir. Cook this over medium heat 10-15 minutes, until bubbly.

Spread the tortilla chips on a lightly greased baking sheet. Top them with the beef mixture then evenly spread the cheese over the top of that. Bake or broil the nachos just until the cheese is melted. Top with desired toppings.

Mini Cheeseburgers

I have to say, I started making these before anyone else (except White Castle, who really was everyone's inspiration with these). They're now quite popular. The most difficult part of this recipe is the bun. I suggest making your own (p. 96). Whole Foods occasionally carries a good brown-and-serve roll, as does Trader Joe's. They're typically available only around certain holidays, but if you ask the store they may be able to get them in for you.

12 brown and serve dinner rolls
1¼# ground beef
3 slices cheddar cheese

Make twelve little burgers out of the ground beef. Lay the patties on a baking sheet and bake the burgers at 375° to the desired doneness (at school I cook them so they're brown all the way through, at home I bake them until pink inside). Cut the rolls in half. Place the bottom halves in a baking dish, top each with a quarter of a slice of cheese and a burger, place the bun-tops on the burgers, and smoosh them down a little. Bake these at 325° for about five minutes. Don't over cook these, as the bread will get too hard.

I sometimes throw a little ranch seasoning into the meat for ranch burgers, or a little taco seasoning for Mexican burgers. Be creative!!

Pizza

A good homemade pizza is such a great way to welcome your kids home from school, and they're nowhere near as difficult to make as you might expect. If you prepare the pizza dough in the morning, you can pull it out of the fridge and throw together a pizza in a few minutes.

Friday can still be pizza night at your house. Instead of ordering the pizza, make it. Pull out the dough that you made last night, and gather the family. There's nothing better than the mixture of fresh food and family laughter in the kitchen. While the pizza's in the oven, throw together a Caesar or Italian salad and throw a fruit cobbler in the oven for later. This will not just make for a happy Friday, it will contribute to a happier, healthier weekend.

pizza dough (p. 91) This recipe is enough for two pizzas.
2 - 4 T. olive oil
3 c. marinara or pizza sauce
3 c. shredded mozzarella cheese
½ c. shredded cheddar cheese
your favorite toppings: I like pineapple pizza, or just banana
                            peppers, but the toppings are
                            completely up to you

When making your pizza dough you can add garlic powder, or ranch mix, if you like.

It's much easier to start with deep-dish pizzas, using two or three 13x9x2 pans. You should have no trouble getting the dough into these pans. Thinner crusts are more difficult, but easily mastered. Don't sweat this process. Pizza dough is very forgiving.

Roll out the pizza dough, pick it up and place it in or on a lightly greased pan. When you pick the dough up it will lose its shape.

Don't worry. Place the dough in or on the pan you're using (it doesn't need to be a pizza pan, you can use a baking sheet). Spread the dough gently with your fingers until it covers the pan. I always keep a little dough aside to use as a hole-patch, as holes will occur.

Once you get really handy with the dough you can try the toss-and-stretch method that I grew up watching (when I was a kid the pizza parlors usually featured access to the pizza chef, who would toss and twirl the pizza dough in the air to achieve the right dimensions. We thought it was really cool).

Brush the dough lightly with olive oil. You can also sprinkle a little basil and/or oregano on the dough. Cover the pie with the sauce, cheeses, and whatever toppings you like. Bake your pizzas at 400° about 8-10 minutes for thin crust, 425° 12-18 minutes for thicker crust. DON'T open the oven door for at least the first eight minutes.

If you want to make calzones, only cover half of the dough with sauce, cheese and toppings, fold it over, and pinch it all the way around, making sure it's completely sealed. Put a few slices in the top to vent (this is very important) and bake at 425° about twenty minutes.

White sauce (alfredo) pizzas are trendy now, and really delish. Here are a few white sauce pizza ideas:

Cover a large (lightly greased) baking sheet with pizza dough and top it with 1½ c. alfredo sauce (p.197). Evenly spread 1# lightly sautéed mushrooms, 1 c. frozen chopped spinach, 1 c. shredded mozzarella and ½ c. shredded provolone over the pie. You can omit the mushrooms, use half of the spinach and add 1 c. chopped chicken for a really great chicken alfredo pizza.

Chicken Roll-Up Sandwiches

4 12" flour tortillas
1# chicken, cooked and diced (I use leftover chicken strips)
1 tomato, diced
1 head romaine lettuce, shredded
1 c. shredded (not grated) parmesan cheese
½ c. ranch dressing

Combine the chicken, lettuce, tomatoes, cheese and ranch dressing, and toss until thoroughly mixed. Place ¼ of the chicken mixture into middle of a tortilla, fold the ends in, and roll it up rather tightly. Cut in half and serve.

Chicken Wraps

4 8" tortillas
8 pieces of chicken (I use leftover chicken fingers)
4 leaves of romaine lettuce
4 whole tomato slices, cut in halves
2 cheese slices
4 T. dressing (I use ranch, but French or honey mustard are good too)

Spread 1 T. dressing in the center of a tortilla. Put half of a cheese slice, a leaf of lettuce, two tomato halves and a chicken finger in the center of a tortilla. Fold the tortilla from the bottom and then from both sides. They're best if the chicken is warm.

Potato Skins

You don't need a deep fryer for these. If you have time to bake potatoes in the morning, you can send the meat of the potato in a hot thermos with a little butter, salt and some veggies, like corn, for lunch, and save the skins for after school.

4 cold baked potatoes
2 t. sunflower oil
½ t. salt
1 c. cheese
1 pc. crumbled bacon (optional)
1 t. chopped scallions or chives (optional)

Cut the baked potatoes in half lengthwise (down the skinny side) and scoop out the potato meat, leaving some on the skin. Using a pastry brush, spread ¼ t. of sunflower oil over the meat side of each skin. Place the skins meat-side up in a baking dish, sprinkle with salt, fill them with the cheese and desired toppings, and bake. You can serve these with sour cream or ranch dip.

Kale Chips

These don't look very appetizing, but they're really good. I got this recipe from my favorite organic farmer, Katie, of Nature's Pace Organic.

4 c. kale
1 T. ranch seasoning (optional)
1 T. olive oil
1 t. salt

Cut the kale into chip-size pieces. Toss the kale with the oil, salt and/or seasoning. Spread them on a lightly greased baking sheet and bake.

Nut Balls

I got this recipe from Katie too. It's easy, tasty and very nutritious. I'm not going to lie, sometimes I drizzle chocolate syrup on these.

2 T. flax seed
1½ t. almond butter
1½ t. honey
2 T. almonds, walnuts or pecans, chopped

In a small mixing bowl combine the almond butter and honey. When this is mixed thoroughly add the nuts and flax seed. Stir to incorporate then shape the mixture into balls.

Fruit Parfaits

These are a great summer treat, and they're so much fun! I make them with berries, but you can use any fruit. If you're using bananas, slice them and soak them in pineapple juice to keep them from browning.

6 oz. yogurt or fruit dip
½ c. granola
¼ c. blueberries
¼ c. strawberries
whipped cream (optional)

Put ¼ c. granola in the bottom of a coffee cup, add a third of the yogurt and spread it over the granola, then add the strawberries and spread them over the yogurt. Add another third of the yogurt, then the blueberries, then the rest of the yogurt, and top this with the remaining granola. A dollop of whipped cream on top adds a little decadence.

Peanut Butter Banana Bake

350° 30 or 40 minutes

Any combination of bananas and syrup is a great snack, I think. A really quick version of this snack is banana slices, drizzled with syrup and topped with nuts.

½ c. peanut butter
3 T. maple syrup or honey
3 bananas
½ t. vanilla
1 c. chopped peanuts
1 c. organic flake cereal, (like corn flakes, wheaties or raisin bran).

Cut the bananas in strips lengthwise and lay them flat in a greased 8x8 pan. Combine the honey or maple syrup, peanut butter and vanilla in a bowl and mix this thoroughly. Pour this mixture over the bananas, then top them with the chopped peanuts and cereal. Cover and bake. Remove the cover about five minutes before you remove the dish from the oven.

Pretzels

450° 12 – 14 minutes

1½ c. hot (115°) water
2 t. brown sugar
2 t. sugar
2 t. salt
1 pkg. (2¼ t.) yeast
4½ c. flour
10 c. water
⅔ c. baking soda
1 egg yolk and 1 T. water
rock salt

Dissolve the sugar in the hot water then sprinkle the yeast over the top. Let this sit for about 5 minutes, stirring gently once, after about 2 minutes. Add the salt and 1 c. flour and stir. Add the remaining flour in 1 c. increments. When the dough is not sticky turn it out onto a floured surface and knead it for about 5 minutes. Place the dough in a lightly greased bowl, turning the dough over to be sure that it is oiled on all sides. Cover the dough ad let it rise in a warm oven (125° – 150°) for an hour. Remove the dough from the warm place, punch it down, and divide it into twelve balls. Form each ball into a rope, and shape each rope into a pretzel. Lay the pretzels on a lightly greased parchment-lined baking sheet. Bring the 10 c. water to boil and add the baking soda. Immerse each pretzel (one at a time) in the boiling water for 30 - 40 seconds then return them to the baking sheet. Lightly beat the egg yolk in a small bowl and mix in the water. Brush each pretzel with the egg yolk mixture, sprinkle rock salt on each, and pop them in the oven.

Ranch Cheese Spread

This is a really quick and simple cheese spread. It's great with crackers, and really good stuffed in celery.

2 T. sour cream
1 T. ranch mix
1 t. minced onion
8 oz. cream cheese
2 c. shredded cheddar cheese
1 c. shredded Mexican blend cheese

Heat the sour cream in a saucepan over low heat. Add the cream cheese and heat this until the cream cheese is melted, stirring often. Add the cheeses, ranch mix and minced onion and heat this until the cheese is melted.

I store this cheese spread in cottage cheese containers. You can omit the ranch mix and add 1 T. Dijon mustard, if you like. The mustard version is really good with pretzels.

Desserts

I think that desserts are a much-maligned part of our diet, mostly because of the sugar, I suspect. While I certainly don't condone huge helpings, especially at night, a little sugar is really not a bad thing. The human body needs 84 grams of sugar per day. If you've cut conventional sodas and cereals from your kids' diets you've already decreased their sugar intake significantly. And desserts don't have to be eaten after dinner. They're great as an after-school or lunchtime snack, and if they incorporate some whole grains, nuts and/or fruit, "desserts" can be a great way to get real food into your children. I try to incorporate whole-wheat flour, and throw in some nuts, especially walnuts, whenever I'm baking. A handful of walnuts a couple of times a week can really contribute to optimum health.

The truth is, kids typically come home from school whipped, and some warm apple crisp or pumpkin bread pudding or spice cake, or any of these desserts that I have served to students for eight years, can make the second part of your child's day happier and more productive. I like desserts after school—again, I know this is contrary to all you've been taught, but really, the bulk of a child's nutritional requirements should already have been met by dinner, and a snack at 4:00 which consists of whole grains, nuts, fruit and yes, sugar (in one of its forms), followed by a lighter dinner, will provide the sustained energy that a child needs. And it won't ruin dinner. When your children are not eating processed foods, enriched flour, high fructose corn syrup or partially hydrogenated oils, and eating real food, they will have more energy, and thus burn more calories, and they will eat their dinner. It's important to stick to the regimen, though, because an empty dinner (one that tastes good but has no nutritional value and lots of additives) can lead to headaches and grouchiness.

No wheat or sugar are really healthy standards, but that's just not do-able for some families, and in this world, it is very, very difficult to keep your child out of mass culture, which is all about fast food, pop, pizza and candy. Offering healthy alternatives to the cultural standards is a beginning, hopefully a means to the end of changing those standards. Not using food as a reward and not eating with our eyes are two important tips. Processed glop is more visually appealing thanks to the white (bleached) flour and intense colors (food dyes made from scary chemicals) that render processed foods more visually enticing than their real counterparts. It may take your child some time to get used to the browner, less pretty appearance of desserts made with real ingredients. Tell them why real food looks different. Talk to them about bleach and chemicals and what's wrong with processed foods. They'll get on board. The browner, less attractive desserts actually taste, and smell, so much better.

Apple Crisp

375° about 45 minutes

This was one of the very first things that I learned to make. The recipe that I now use is really a cross between that first recipe of my grandmother's and Shana's, which the kids at the Waldorf school adored.

One of my favorite things about the Waldorf school was the way that small children prepared their daily snack. It was a part of their day. I believe that food preparation should be an integral part of each child's day, beginning as soon as they can use a spoon. Children need to be connected to the food process. They need to see, and know, real food. Apple crisp is an easy way to incorporate food preparation. A four year old could cut apples with a plastic knife. Though you would need to peel and core the apples, and cut the butter, children can pretty much make an apple crisp on their own. And the smell alone is enough to make them feel good about the work they've done.

6 apples, peeled and diced
1 t. water
½ t. whole-wheat flour
⅛ t. sea salt
¼ c. sugar (you can use maple syrup)
1 t. cinnamon

¼ c. flour
¼ c. whole-wheat flour
1½ c. oats
1 c. brown sugar
½ c. butter
¼ t. cinnamon

In a mixing bowl, combine the flour, sea salt, sugar and cinnamon. Add the apples. Drizzle the water over the apples and toss this, then pour the apple mixture into a greased baking dish. In a separate (or the same) bowl combine and mix all of the topping ingredients except the butter. Cut in the butter using a pastry blender or two butter knives. Cover the apples with the topping and bake until bubbly.

Cranberry Crisp

375° about 40 minutes

This is one of my sister's favorite desserts.

4 apples, peeled and diced
3 pears, peeled and diced
2½ c. fresh or frozen cranberries
¾ c. sugar
juice of one orange

Topping:

½ c. flour
½ c. whole-wheat flour
1½ c. oats
1 c. brown sugar
½ c. butter
¼ t. nutmeg
¼ c. chopped walnuts (optional)

Chop the cranberries in the food processor, and mix ¾ c. sugar into the chopped cranberries. In a mixing bowl combine the apples, pears, orange juice and cranberry mixture and stir to mix. Spread the fruit mixture in a greased baking dish. In a separate (or the same) bowl combine all of the topping ingredients except the butter and mix. Cut in the butter, cover the fruit mixture with the topping, and bake.

Lazy Daisy Cake

350° 25 minutes

This is one of my all time, and very first, favorites. I sell these at the farmers markets occasionally. I use this cake as the base for my strawberry shortcake, and when doing special occasion cakes, I layer this cake with a strawberry filling in between the layers and cover it with either homemade butter-cream icing or whipped cream.

1 c. milk
2 T. butter, melted
2 c. flour
2 t. baking powder
½ t. salt
4 eggs
2 c. sugar
2½ t. vanilla

Melt the butter in a saucepan and add the milk. Heat the milk and butter to about 130° degrees. In a mixing bowl combine the dry ingredients. In a separate bowl beat the eggs and the vanilla for about two minutes, until thick. Add the sugar and beat another minute. Add the egg mixture to the dry ingredients and mix thoroughly. Have your baking pan ready, because you need to move quickly once you add the warm milk to the batter. Once the batter is smooth add the milk to the batter, stirring to incorporate. Pour the batter into a 13x9x2 pan and bake.

6 T. butter
½ c. brown sugar
2 T. heavy cream
¾ c. coconut
¼ c. pecans (optional)

Melt the butter in a saucepan. Add the remaining ingredients and mix thoroughly. When the cake is golden brown and springs back when touched in the center remove it from the oven, spread the topping over the cake, and return it to the oven, baking it for a few (5 – 10) more minutes, until the topping is just beginning to brown. Allow the cake to cool before cutting.

Apple Cake

400° 40 minutes

This is a moist and gooey cake. This cake is good served at room temperature. I usually bake it the day before I'm going to serve it and refrigerate it, then bring it back to room temperature before serving.

1 c. flour
¾ c. sugar
2 T. baking powder
¼ t. sea salt
1 t. vanilla
4 eggs, lightly beaten
4 T. sunflower oil
⅔ c. milk
8 apples, cored, peeled and cut in wedges

The Topping:

⅔ c. sugar
½ t. cinnamon
2 eggs, lightly beaten
6 T. melted butter
½ t. vanilla

In a large bowl combine the flour, sugar, baking powder and sea salt. Add the eggs, oil and vanilla and mix. Add the milk and stir until well blended. Add the apples. Spread this mixture in a buttered 13x9x2 pan and bake until firm, about twenty-five minutes. In a small bowl combine the topping ingredients and mix thoroughly. Remove the cake from the oven and spread the topping mixture over it. Return it to the oven and bake until the topping is bubbly and the cake is firm to the touch, about ten more minutes.

Strawberry Shortcake

lazy daisy cake, cut in squares
2# strawberries
strawberry glaze
whipped cream (p.245)

<u>The Glaze:</u>

¾ c. strawberries, quartered (these can be frozen strawberries)
1 c. water
¼ c. sugar
⅓ c. strawberry jelly

In a saucepan heat the water, sugar, and strawberries to boiling. Let this mixture cook for about fifteen minutes, then add the jelly. You can puree the strawberries if you like (I do). I usually puree them with a hand macerator before I add the jelly. After adding the jelly heat on medium for another minute or two. Remove it from the heat and allow it to cool, stirring occasionally.

To prepare your strawberry shortcake add the remaining strawberries to the strawberry glaze and toss lightly. Spoon the strawberries onto the cake squares and top this with homemade whipped cream.

Whipped Cream

1 c. heavy cream, chilled
1½ t. sugar
½ t. vanilla

The key to good homemade whipped cream is temperature. Don't try to whip cream in a hot kitchen, and you should always put your bowl and beaters in the freezer for at least 15 minutes before preparation.

Beat the cream in a cold bowl for one minute. While beating the cream slowly add the sugar. Continue to beat another two minutes then add the vanilla. Beat this until peaks form.

Berry Cake

This is great when the berries come in season. I love it with homemade whipped cream on a summer night.

3 c. flour
2 t. baking powder
½ t. salt
1 c. butter
1½ + ½ c. sugar
4 eggs, separated
2½ t. vanilla
2 c. fresh or frozen blueberries
1¼ c. fresh or frozen raspberries

Combine and mix the dry ingredients. In a separate bowl beat the butter and 1½ c. sugar with an electric mixture until creamed (two or three minutes). Add the egg yolks and the vanilla and beat another minute. In a different bowl beat the egg whites on high speed for two minutes. Gradually add the ½ c. sugar and beat until stiff, about 4 minutes. Combine the dry ingredients with the egg yolk mixture and beat until smooth. Fold in the egg whites, then add the fruit and stir lightly. Pour the batter into lightly greased 13x9x2 pan and bake.

Spice Cake

350° about 30 minutes

This was a favorite at the Waldorf school. My very good friend Cindy always brought it in for her son's birthday celebration. It makes a nice mini cupcake, too. You can top this with a dollop of cream cheese frosting (p. 256) or just confectioner's sugar, or nothing, really.

1 c. whole-wheat flour
1 c. flour
1 c. sugar
2 t. cinnamon
1 t. baking soda
½ t. salt
½ t. ground nutmeg
¼ t. allspice
1 egg
1 t. vanilla
¼ c. sunflower oil
1½ c. applesauce
1 c. golden raisins (optional)

Mix the dry ingredients. In a separate bowl beat the egg. Add the vanilla and the oil and beat again for about 30 seconds. Stir in the applesauce. Add the applesauce mixture to the dry ingredients and mix thoroughly. Pour the batter into a greased or paper-lined 13x9x2 pan and bake.

Pumpkin Cake

350° about 30 minutes

Color me weird, but I love whipped cream with my pumpkin cake. I serve it naked at school, but it's also good with cream cheese frosting.

2 eggs
1½ c. fresh pumpkin puree
1 c. brown sugar
½ c. sunflower oil
½ t. salt
1 t. baking soda
2 t. baking powder
1½ t. cinnamon
¼ t. ginger
½ t. cloves
¾ t. nutmeg
⅔ c. milk
1¼ c. flour
¼ c. whole-wheat flour

Mix the dry ingredients. In a separate bowl beat the eggs for a minute, then add the pumpkin, brown sugar, eggs and oil and mix thoroughly. Add the pumpkin mixture to the dry ingredients then stir in the milk. Pour the batter into a greased 13x9x2 pan and bake.

Walnut Cake

350° 20-25 minutes

I top this with almond whipped cream (substitute the vanilla in the homemade whipped cream with pure almond extract).

¼ c. whole-wheat flour
1¼ c. flour
1 t. baking soda
½ t. salt
1 T. butter
1 T. almond butter (If you don't have almond butter around, skip it, and use 2 T. butter)
1 c. sugar
1 egg
1½ t. vanilla
½ c. milk or half and half
¾ c. chopped walnuts

Mix the dry ingredients together in a mixing bowl. In a separate bowl beat the butter and almond butter until combined. Add the sugar and beat until creamed, about two minutes. Add the egg and vanilla and beat another minute. Add the butter mixture and the walnuts to the dry ingredients. Slowly add the milk and beat this until smooth. Pour the batter into a greased 13x9x2 pan and bake.

Jelly Bars

350° 35 minutes

1½ c. flour
¼ c. whole-wheat flour
1¼ c. oats
1 c. brown sugar
¾ c. butter
1 c. jelly (I like cherry, but apricot or strawberry are also good.)
¼ c. chopped pecans or walnuts (optional)

In a mixing bowl combine the first four ingredients. Cut in the butter. In a greased 9x9 pan spread ¾ of the oat mixture and pat it down until it's firm. Top this with the jelly, then sprinkle the remaining oat mixture and nuts over top. Press this down just a bit and pop it in the oven.

PBJ Bars

1 c. flour
½ c. whole-wheat flour
1½ c. oats
1 c. brown sugar
¼ c. butter
½ c. peanut butter
½ c. chopped peanuts
1 10 oz. jar jelly (I like Trader Joe's Super Fruit myself)

Combine the first four ingredients. Cut in the butter and peanut butter. In a greased 9x9 pan spread ¾ of the peanut butter mixture then pat this down to make a crust. Spread the jelly on top of the crust. Sprinkle the remaining peanut butter mixture and the chopped peanuts on top of that, press this down just a bit, and bake. Allow this to cool a little before cutting.

Lemon Squares

350° 15-18 minutes, then another 25 minutes

These were a huge hit at the Waldorf school. One of my very favorite students called them little pieces of heaven. They're very popular at the school I'm now at as well, especially among the teachers. I have one very special family who buys a tray of these each month when I make them.

The Crust:

¾ c. flour
¼ c. whole-wheat flour
¼ c. confectioner's sugar
½ c. butter

The Topping:

2 eggs
1 c. sugar
¼ c. lemon juice
2 T. flour
½ t. baking powder
½ t. lemon rind

To make the crust mix the first four ingredients together, then cut in the butter. Press the crust mixture firmly into a greased 9x9 pan and bake this for 15-18 minutes, until it's very lightly browned. In the same bowl mix the topping ingredients and beat this lightly for about 30 seconds. Remove the crust from the oven and pour the lemon mixture over the crust. Bake this for another 25 minutes.

Butterscotch Brownies

375° 30 minutes

The eighth grade class at the Waldorf school LOVED these. They were a great class, and were very appreciative of my cooking. They were also very kind and helpful to me, much to many of the administrators' chagrin. A warm plate of yummy brownies goes a long way.

1½ c. flour
½ c. oats
½ t. salt
1 t. baking soda
⅛ t. cinnamon
1 c. butter
1 c. brown sugar
½ c. sugar
2 eggs
1 t. vanilla

In a mixing bowl combine the dry ingredients. In a separate bowl cream the sugar, brown sugar and butter for about 90 seconds. Add the eggs and the vanilla and beat another 30 seconds. Add the butter mixture to the dry ingredients and mix thoroughly. Spread the batter (it will be thick) in a lightly greased 9x9 pan and bake.

Pineapple Carrot Cake

350° 55 minutes

2 c. flour
½ c. whole-wheat flour
2 t. baking soda
1 t. salt
2 t. cinnamon
½ c. sunflower
3 eggs
2 c. sugar
2 t. vanilla
1¼ c. shredded carrots
1 c. crushed pineapple, drained
½ c. coconut (optional)
½ c. chopped walnuts (optional)

Combine the dry ingredients. In a separate bowl beat the eggs and the vanilla for about a minute. Add the sugar and beat another minute. Add the oil and mix thoroughly. Add the carrots, pineapple and coconut. Add this mixture to the dry ingredients and stir until mixed. Pour this into a lightly greased 13x9x2 pan and bake. I top this cake with powdered sugar when it's cool.

Carrot Cake

375° 40-45 minutes

2½ c. flour
2 t. baking powder
½ t. salt
1 t. cinnamon
¼ t. ginger
½ t. nutmeg
1 c. butter
2 c. sugar
4 eggs
1½ t. vanilla
1 c. milk
1½ c. shredded carrots
½ c. walnuts or pecans (optional)

Combine and mix the dry ingredients. Add the carrots. In a separate bowl beat the butter and sugar for about 90 seconds. Add the eggs and the vanilla and beat another minute. Blend together the egg and carrot mixtures then gradually add the milk and the nuts. Beat this until it's smooth. Pour the batter into a greased 13x9x2 pan and bake. When the cake is cool top it with cream cheese frosting (p.256).

Cream Cheese Frosting

2 T. butter, softened
4 T. cream cheese, softened
2 c. confectioner's sugar
½ t. vanilla

In a small bowl whip the butter and cream cheese with an electric mixer at high speed about 2 minutes. Add the confectioner's sugar (stirring it in gently) and vanilla and beat well.

Mini Tarts

I have this really cool tool (they sell them at kitchen or cake decorating stores) that makes these cute little tart shells. You put a ball of dough in each mini muffin indenture (they also make cupcake-sized tools, so you can use cupcake or mini-muffin pans) and press down with the tool and it makes a perfect little shell. I serve apple and cherry tarts at school frequently.

1½ c. flour
½ c. whole-wheat flour
1 t. salt
½ c. butter, chilled
⅓ c. ice cold water

In a food processor combine the dry ingredients. Add the butter and pulse the processor about 15 times. Drizzle the iced water in while pulsing the food processor. It won't form a ball, but will form small crumbles. Form small dough balls with your hands. Place the dough balls in the mini-muffin or cupcake pans and smoosh them down with the tart tool. Bake at 400° for about 12 minutes.

For more of a cookie-like crust, try these tart shells:

1 c. butter
½ c. sugar
2 c. flour
⅛ t. salt

Cream the butter, sugar and salt. Stir in the flour. Form small balls of dough, place one in each cupcake or mini-muffin indenture,

and smoosh them down with the tart tool. Bake at 325° for about
fifteen minutes. Cool and fill.

Cherry Filling

2 c. cherries (if you're using frozen thaw them and use the water/
        juice that is in the package)
2 T. maple syrup or sugar
1½ c. water or juice from the cherries
2 T. cherry jelly
2½ T. cornstarch
¼ c. water
½ t. almond extract
¼ t. vanilla

Cook the cherries, syrup or sugar and water/juice in a saucepan over medium heat until it begins to boil. Add the jelly and stir for a minute or two. Mix the cornstarch with the water and add this to the cherry mixture. Bring to a boil and stir for one minute, then remove it from the heat. Stir in the almond and the vanilla, and allow the mixture to cool slightly.

Apple Filling

6 c. apples, skinned, cored and diced
2 c. organic apple cider or juice
2 T. maple syrup or sugar
2 t. cinnamon
2 – 3 T. cornstarch
¼ c. water
1 T. butter

Cook the apples in the cider or juice. When the apples begin to soften add the cinnamon and syrup or sugar and simmer, covered, until the apples are tender, about 20 minutes. Mix the cornstarch and the water and add this to the apple mixture. Stir, while boiling, one minute. Remove the apples from the heat and let them cool for about five minutes. Stir in the butter.

Fruit and Pudding Bars

Okay, this is one that I cheat on. Organic or all-natural pudding is really not very expensive or hard to come by, and custard or pudding from scratch is a bit too laborious for me. In an attempt not to eat all of my leftover cookies I freeze them and pull them out to make this crust. Just toss a few in the food processor. Top cookie crumbles with fruit and you have an easy-peasy dessert. I like to use the apple or cherry filling as the fruit layer. Adding some maple-roasted almonds, walnuts or pecans makes this a complete snack. You don't have to bake the crust if you don't want to, and you can also make these into individual treats, using dessert dishes or even paper cups. If you're preparing individual desserts a dollop of whipped cream is lovely.

Crust:

3 c. cookie crumbs
½ c. softened or melted butter

Combine the crumbs and the butter and press the mixture into a greased 9x9 pan. Bake at 400° for about 10 minutes. Allow the crust to cool before you top it.

Topping:

2 c. organic pudding or 1½ c. whipped cream
1 c. fruit filling

Some fun fruit and pudding bar ideas:

Apple Bars

Use snickerdoodles (cinnamon sugar cookies) for the crust. Top with a layer of butterscotch or vanilla pudding and top that with apple pie filling.

Cherry Royale Bars

Use vanilla sugar cookies for the crust and vanilla pudding and cherry pie filling as toppings.

PBJ Bars

Use peanut butter cookies, top with peanut or almond butter, cherry filling or fruit jelly and vanilla or butterscotch pudding.

Peppermint Patties

You may have noticed that there isn't much chocolate here. See my notes on caffeine. Yes, there's caffeine in chocolate, and as such, I do not serve it at school. The peppermint patty was the one exception to that rule. I made them up individually in plastic cocktail cups and served them on the last day before Christmas vacation for a few years. The school has now asked parents to forego chocolate, so I don't serve these at school anymore, but I make them up at home. They're a quick and really delish holiday treat. If you have a festive holiday glass or dessert cup you can make them up individually.

1 box chocolate mint cookies (organic or all natural are actually readily available)
2 c. organic chocolate pudding
2 c. organic vanilla pudding
whipped cream
organic candy canes, crushed

Layer the crumbled cookies, vanilla pudding and chocolate pudding in a 9x9 pan or in individual dishes. Top with whipped cream and crushed candy canes.

Bread Pudding

I love bread puddings. They are an easy way to use up any uneaten bread, and there are a plethora of varieties. To properly cook a bread pudding you need to employ a water bath (place pudding pan in a larger pan and add an inch or so of water to the larger/outer pan) and cook the bread pudding slowly (75 minutes or so). This method does lend more of a pudding consistency, but cooking it in a baking dish at 350° will work as well—your pudding will be less custard-y and more bread-y, if you will.

I mix the custard mixture in a stand up blender.

Blueberry Bread Pudding

350 ° 45 minutes

4 slices sandwich bread, crusts removed
2 c. bread pieces (including the bread crusts, cut or torn into pieces)
3 eggs
2 c. cream, half and half or whole milk
1 c. sugar or ¾ c. maple syrup
1 t. vanilla
1 c. fresh or frozen blueberries
1 T. butter

Butter one side of each slice of bread. In a mixing bowl or blender combine the eggs and the sugar. Beat this for about 30 seconds then add the cream and the vanilla. Spread the bread pieces in a 9x9 baking dish, top with the blueberries, then fit the slices, buttered side down, over the top. Pour the egg mixture over the bread, cover with foil and bake. Remove the foil after about thirty minutes. You can substitute bananas for the blueberries, or to make a Hawaiian treat use crushed pineapple and sprinkle the top with coconut.

Pecan Raisin Bread Pudding

350° 45 – 50 minutes

2½ c. bread pieces
3 eggs
2 c. cream, half and half or whole milk
1 c. sugar or ¾ c. maple syrup
½ t. vanilla
1½ t. cinnamon
1 c. raisins

Topping

½ c. pecans
¼ c. brown sugar or 2 T. maple syrup
2 T. softened or melted butter

Spread the bread pieces in a greased 9x9 baking dish. Beat the eggs and the sugar together for about thirty seconds, then add the cream, vanilla and cinnamon and blend. Sprinkle the raisins over the bread and pour the egg mixture over this. Toss the pecans in the butter and syrup or brown sugar and spread them over the bread. Cover the bread pudding with foil and bake. Remove the foil after about 40 minutes.

Pumpkin Bread Pudding

350° 1 hour

If you have leftover pumpkin bread around throw it in this bread pudding. I usually serve this cold with whipped cream.

4 slices bread, crusts removed, buttered on one side
2 c. bread pieces (you can use leftover pumpkin bread for this if you
             like)
3 eggs
1 c. cream, half and half or whole milk
1 c. sugar or ¾ c. maple syrup
1½ c. fresh pumpkin puree
1 t. cinnamon
½ t. fresh grated nutmeg
⅛ t. ground cloves
½ t. vanilla

Spread the bread pieces evenly in a greased 9x9 pan. Fit the bread slices snugly on top, buttered sides down. Beat the eggs and sugar or syrup for a minute then add the remaining ingredients and mix thoroughly. Pour the pumpkin mixture over the bread and bake, covered with foil. Remove the foil after about 45 minutes.

Mini Cheesecakes

400° 16-18 minutes

These are so cute and quick. I prefer using the mini muffin pans for these, but you can do them in cupcake pans, too. The organic mini vanilla wafers are a perfect fit in the mini muffin pans, and most organic vanilla wafers will work in the cupcake pans.

I top mine with a drop (usually one cherry) of cherry filling, but they're great plain. You can also top them with fresh strawberries or strawberry topping. To make turtle cheesecakes top with a few mini chocolate chips right after removing them from the oven, and when they're cool drizzle with a drop of caramel sauce.

18 organic vanilla wafers or 48 organic mini vanilla wafers
32 oz. organic cream cheese, softened
½ c. sugar
2 eggs
½ t. vanilla
½ t. pure almond extract

Whip the cream cheese with an electric mixer at high speed for about two minutes. Add the sugar and the eggs and beat this for another 45 seconds. Add the vanilla and almond and mix thoroughly. Place one cookie, round side up, in each muffin cup (I always use the paper liners). Fill each about ¼ full with the cream cheese mixture and bake.

Fruit Cobbler

375° 40 – 50 minutes

This is the easiest cobbler recipe I know. You need to adjust the butter quantity a bit, depending on what kind of fruit you use. A big cheat is using a store-bought organic cake mix instead of actually preparing the cobbler mix yourself.

1 c. flour
¼ c. whole-wheat flour
1 c. sugar
½ t. salt
1 egg, lightly beaten
½ c. melted butter

Combine the first four ingredients. Cut in the egg. Spread the fruit or fruit mixture in a greased 9x9 pan then spread the cobbler mix evenly over the fruit. Drizzle the melted butter over the top and bake until bubbly.

Peach cobbler

Toss 2 c. sliced peaches with the juice of ½ lemon and 1 t. sugar or ¾ t. maple syrup. You can add some lemon zest to the cobbler mix for extra zing.

Cherry cobbler

Toss 16 oz. cherries with 1 t. sugar or ½ t. maple syrup and ½ t. almond extract. These will just cook to liquid, so back off on the butter a bit and don't overcook.

Apple cobbler

Toss 2 c. peeled apple slices with 1 t. sugar or ¾ t. maple syrup and 1 t. cinnamon. You can add ½ t. of cinnamon and a dash of nutmeg to the cobbler mix for extra yumminess.

Pumpkin Cobbler

350° 40 minutes

This has replaced pumpkin pie as the Thanksgiving dessert in my house. For this one I employ the cheat and use cake mix. Some organic cake mixes only make a 9x9 cake, and if this is the case, use two.

2 c. pureed pumpkin
3 eggs
1 c. half and half or whipping cream
1 c. sugar (you can use half white and half brown if you like)
⅛ t. salt
¾ t. ginger
2 t. cinnamon
½ t. nutmeg
1 t. vanilla
1 white or yellow cake mix
1½ c. butter
1 c. chopper pecans (optional)

Combine the first nine ingredients and mix thoroughly. Pour this mixture into a 13x9x2 pan. Sprinkle the cake mix over the top, then drizzle the butter over that. Pop it in the oven for about 25 minutes, remove and top with the nuts, and bake it for 15 more minutes.

Pumpkin Pie

2 c. pureed pumpkin
¼ c. light corn syrup
½ c. brown sugar
3 eggs
1 c. cream
1½ t. cinnamon
½ t. salt
½ t. nutmeg
dash cloves
2 piecrusts (p. 273)

Prepare two 9" piecrusts. Mix all of that stuff together, pour it into the piecrusts, and bake.

Piecrust

I like to use the food processor to make piecrust, but you can use a basic pastry blender or two knives. If you're using the processor the butter needs to be cold and you can, of course, make this with some (or all) whole-wheat flour.

½ c. butter
2 c. flour
1 t. salt
⅓ c. iced water

Combine the flour and salt. Cut in the butter. Drizzle the iced water over the dough mixture. You want the dough to just hold together (you don't want it to be sticky).

On a floured surface roll the dough out into a circle, fold it in half, and place it in your pie pan. Unfold, fit and fill.

Almond Cookies

350° 10 minutes

These are so good and so simple. The school that I'm at now is nut free, so I can't serve them there, but they were a staple at the Waldorf school.

2¼ c. flour
1 c. butter
½ c. sugar
1 t. vanilla extract
1 t. almond extract
½ c. chopped almonds

Cream the butter and the sugar together. Add the extracts and blend well. Add the flour and the nuts and mix thoroughly. Drop the dough by spoonfuls onto a lightly greased or parchment- lined pan and bake.

Oatmeal Coconut Cookies

325° 10 minutes

These are a big hit at my current school, so I make them frequently. They were the particular favorite of one of my very favorite students, Charlotte, who graduated two years ago. I miss her.

2 c. flour
1 c. oats
1 t. baking soda
¼ t. salt
1½ c. organic coconut
1 c butter
1 c. sugar
1 c. brown sugar
1 t. vanilla
½ t. almond extract

Cream the butter and sugars. Add the egg and beat well, then add the extracts. In a separate bowl combine the dry ingredients, including the coconut. Add the butter mixture to the dry ingredients and mix well. Drop the dough by spoonfuls onto a parchment-lined baking sheet, smoosh the cookies down a bit, and bake.

African Peanut Banana Cake

350° about 30 minutes

I made this as a dessert for an international food festival at my daughter's high school, and it was a big hit.

1¾ c. flour
¼ c. whole-wheat flour
¼ t. salt
2 t. baking powder
⅔ c. butter
¾ c. sugar
2 eggs
4 bananas
1 cup chopped peanuts

Cream the butter and sugar. Add the eggs and mix thoroughly. Add the bananas and mix until the bananas are smooshed. In a separate bowl mix together the dry ingredients. Add half of the peanuts and the banana mixture to the dry ingredients and stir. Pour the batter into a greased or paper lined 13x9x2 pan, top with the remaining peanuts, and bake.

Easy Macaroons

350° 10 – 12 minutes

2 c. grated coconut
1 can (14 oz.) sweetened condensed milk (yes, they now make
organic)
1 t. vanilla
½ t. almond extract
1 c. pecans

Mix, spoon onto a pan, and bake. How simple is that?

Rice Pudding

¼ c. brown rice
½ c. white rice
5 c. milk
½ c. maple syrup
1 t. vanilla
1 egg yolk

Heat 3 cups of milk in a saucepan over medium heat for about ten minutes. Add the brown rice, bring to a boil, reduce the heat and cook for 15 minutes. Add the white rice and cook for another 30 minutes. Add one cup of milk, the maple syrup and the vanilla and cook for another 15 minutes. Add the last cup of milk and cook for a few more minutes. You need to stir this occasionally to keep the rice from sticking to the bottom of the pan, and you may need to add more milk as it is absorbed by the rice. When it's done (it should still be a little soupy) add the egg yolk and cook for a few more minutes. You can omit the egg, but it adds to the "pudding" consistency.

Pumpkin Oatmeal Cookies

350° about 12 minutes

2½ c. flour
2 c. oats
1 t. baking soda
½ t. baking powder
½ t. salt
2½ t. pumpkin pie spice
½ t. cinnamon
1 c. butter
1 c. brown sugar
½ c. sugar
2 T. honey
1 c. pumpkin puree
1 egg
1½ t. vanilla

In a large mixing bowl combine the flour, oats, baking soda, baking powder, salt and spices. In a separate bowl cream the sugars, butter and honey until light and fluffy. Add the eggs, the pumpkin and the vanilla and mix thoroughly. Mix the pumpkin mixture with the dry ingredients until completely incorporated. Drop the dough by spoonfuls onto a parchment-lined baking tray and bake until golden. Serve these with apple cider on a fall afternoon and you will make friends and influence people. Seriously.

Beverages

This is a very short chapter. I wasn't going to include these, but my dear friend Holly, who created the Fiddlebump Apothecary line, was visiting one day and I made her a strawberry lemonade and she told me that I had to include the recipe in this book. These are offered as a means of ridding your family of conventional pop (yes, if you hadn't guessed, I hail from the Great Lakes State). Letting your children create their own soda will help them get off that insipid colored poison that Americans consume at a sickening rate. Including maple syrup, especially grade B, makes the drink a virtual meal, as maple syrup is so nutritious and sustaining.

Lemon soda

2 T. lemon juice
2 T. maple syrup
1 c. sparkling water

Mix the lemon juice and syrup then add the soda.

Strawberry Lemonade

4 large fresh or frozen organic strawberries
2 T. maple syrup
1½ T. lemon juice
1 c. water or ¾ c. water and a few ice cubes

Put everything in a blender and turn it on.

The Arnold

---

2 T. lemon juice
1 t. maple syrup
½ c. decaf iced tea

    Mix and serve.

Frozen Raspberry Arnold

¼ c. fresh or frozen raspberries
1 t. lemon juice
1 t. maple syrup
¾ c. decaf iced tea

Mix the tea, lemon juice and syrup in a 9 oz. paper cup. Add the raspberries. Put the cup in the freezer. I like a spoon frozen in this, and I'm not crazy about plastic, so I wait until it's slushy then I insert an iced tea spoon into the cup. You can just use a plastic one, or a Popsicle stick. When it's frozen remove it from the cup. It's good to keep the cup for when it starts to get melty.

Cherry Soda

1 T. red tart cherry juice concentrate
1 t. maple syrup
¼ t. almond extract
12 oz. soda

Mix and serve.

Ginger Ale

I cook up a batch of ginger water using fresh ginger for this.

½ c. ginger water
2 t. maple syrup
juice of ½ lime
1½ c. sparkling water

Mix and serve.

<u>Ginger Water:</u>

1 ginger root
4 c. water

Cut the ginger root into 6 or 7 pieces (make sure the root is good and clean). Bring the water and ginger root to a boil, reduce the heat and simmer for 45 – 60 minutes.
If the fragrance of the steeping ginger root makes you want to go shopping don't be surprised. "They" say that the smell of ginger makes people want to spend money.

Recipe Index

Acknowledgements

There is no way that I could accurately account for every source that contributed to the information or recipes in this book.

When I was just beginning my personal food journey, the summer after my mother died, I bought a copy of "The Great American Detox Diet" by Alex Jamieson, (Rodale, 2005) who was at the time the girlfriend of Morgan Spurlock ("Super Size Me") and is a Holistic Health Counselor and Gourmet Natural Foods Chef. That was really my springboard. I then watched the DVD documentary "The Future of Food", (Lily Films, 2004) and from there I was pretty much off to the races. I read articles, pored through websites, and watched applicable TV programs, in an effort to learn as much as I could about the food that I, and We, had been consuming. Some of these TV shows were "Jamie Oliver's Food Revolution", "Dr. Phil", "The Dr. Oz Show", "The Doctors", "Rachel Ray", "NBC Nightly News", "Anderson Cooper 360" and "Real Time with Bill Maher".

I also did quite a bit of networking, at school, with my Waldorf friends, at Whole Foods and Trader Joe's, and particularly at the farmers markets, where I gleaned quiet a bit of info from some very knowledgeable, friendly, generous and kind vendors, all of whom I thank wholeheartedly.

My sister has always been an organic, natural-health kind of girl, and I've gotten quite a bit of info (and support) from her, and I thank her too.

There's (thankfully) a wealth of information concerning the Real Food Revolution out there, on the web, on TV and in print. I wish that I could list (or even recall) every source that has influenced me. Though I can't, I can gratefully salute every soldier in this very worthwhile (and still uphill) battle, for whatever they have contributed to the cause of righting the way we, as a nation, eat.

1. Nelson, Willie. Interview with Larry King, Larry King Live. CNN. 15 April 2010

2. www.treelight.com/health/nutrition/ PartiallyHydrogenatedOils.html

3. Cooper, Ann and Holmes, Lisa M., Lunch Lessons, (New York, Harper Collins Publishers, 2006)

4. Pollen, Michael, The Omnivore's Dilemma (New York: Penguin, 2006)

5. www.disabilityscoop.com/2011/05/23

6. www.vaccinationnews.com/scandals/ feb_15_02_skyrocketing_autism.htm

7. Baughman, Fred A. Jr., MD 9/25/00, www.ritalindeath.com/ adhd.htm

8. Conley, Mikaela, www.abcnews.go.com/Health/adhd-cases-rise

9. www.CDC.gov/nchs/data

10. Chan, Amanda, www.msnbc.com/id/39798848/ns/health-diabetes

11. www.sleepedia.com/sleep-depravation-statistics/

12. www.healthydepressionstrategies.com.html

13. www.drowsydriving.org/about/facts-and-stats

14. Maas, Dr. James B., Power Sleep: The Revolutionary Program That Prepares Your Mind for Peak Performance, (New York: Harper Collins Publishers, 1998)

15. Maas, Dr. James B.

16. Maas, Dr. James B.

17. "Sleep Health" University of Houston, Clear Lake, prtl.uhcl.edu/portal/page/portal/cos/self_help_and_Handouts/Files

18. www.holistic-wellness-basics.com/dehydration.html

19. www.science.howstuffworks.com/caffeine.htm

20. www.wikihow.com/Avoid-High-Fructose-Corn-Syrup

21. www.Treelight.com/health/nurtrition/PartiallyHydrogenatedOils.htm

22. www.globalhealingcenter.com/natural-health/enriched-white-flour

23. www.wikipedia.org/wiki/Genetically-Modified_Food

24. www.sustainabletable.org/getinvolved/materials/rBGH_Handout.pdf

25. www.Shirleys-wellness-café.com/bgh.htm

26. www.knowtify.net/2005USPestIndReptExecSum.pdf

15541546R00162

Made in the USA
Charleston, SC
08 November 2012